1⁰⁰
FVL

20TH CENTURY
GLASS

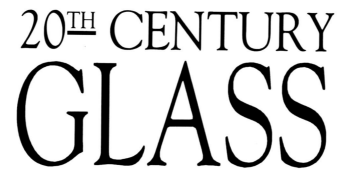

20ᴛʜ CENTURY
GLASS

MARK COUSINS

CHARTWELL
BOOKS, INC.

A QUINTET BOOK

Published by Chartwell Books
A Division of Book Sales, Inc.
110 Enterprise Avenue
Secaucus, New Jersey 07094

ISBN 1-55521-459-2

This book was designed and produced by
Quintet Publishing Limited
6 Blundell Street
London N7 9BH

Creative Director: Peter Bridgewater
Art Director: Ian Hunt
Designer: Sara Nunan
Project Editor: Shaun Barrington
Editor: Henrietta Wilkinson
Picture Researcher: Vivien Adelman

Typeset in Great Britain by
Central Southern Typesetters, Eastbourne
Manufactured in Hong Kong by
Regent Publishing Services Limited
Printed in Hong Kong by
Leefung-Asco Printers Limited

DEDICATION

For Ian, who brought order out of chaos.

Contents

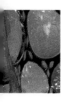

Introduction

Heavy goblet (c.1830) from the
workshops of Bohemia, wheel-cut
and engraved over a combination of
yellow and red stains with silvered
overlay.

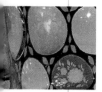

Glass is arguably one of the most misunderstood mediums occupying that somewhat nebulous region between the fine and the applied arts. If questioned on what might be classified as '20th-century glass', many might suggest a Tiffany lampshade, or perhaps a Lalique scent bottle; many more might suggest a snow-scene paperweight or even a straight-sided Guinness glass. Such a narrow range of opinion reflects the somewhat myopic attitude towards glass which has too often been marginalized by the ill-informed as one of the 'lesser' decorative art forms. This book is intended to dispel this misconception and affirm the important contribution glass has made to the development of 20th-century culture. The reproductions contained in this book will hopefully convince even the most sceptical reader. For the uninitiated, even the most cursory investigation into any book on modern glass will reveal a wealth of unknown treasures and surprises.

Unfortunately, the unique skills of the glassmaker have been largely passed over by many mainstream art critics and historians; each month heralds the publication of numerous detailed monographs and erudite analyses on the work of talented painters or architects, but in com-parison books on modern day glass artists are few and far between. This volume is in some small way an attempt to redress this imbalance for the general, art-loving public and to draw its attention to the expansive range of this most malleable of mediums. This book concentrates on the development of glassware and, to a lesser extent, stained glass and glass sculpture, over the past hundred years. Despite being broad in scope, however, it is by no means exhaustive. Although the *objet d'art* is rarely at the forefront of the avant-garde, it has made a valuable contribution to successive genres. To reflect this fact, the book's chapter headings parallel the major artistic movements of the 20th century. Restrictions of space, however, have necessitated the adoption of a rigorous selection procedure, which has meant that many of the more peripheral, though nonetheless meritorious, artists have had to be omitted to allow enough space to concentrate on the most important figures from each particular period. This editing process has been partly subjective and by no means an easy task. But I make no apologies for my particular prejudices and hope that this selection will awaken other people's curiosity to what is one of the most exciting mediums in the decorative arts today.

(RIGHT) *An intricate arrangement of bowls within bowls, each delicately laced with coloured threads of contrasting colours, by Dale Chihuly.*

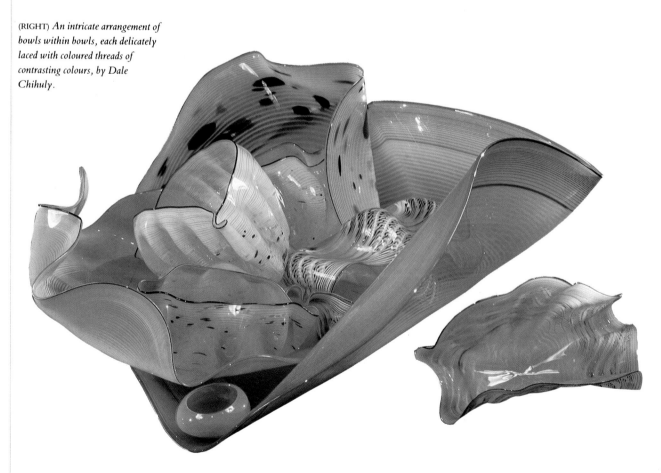

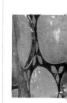

(LEFT) *Vase (1917) by Emile Gallé;
his consummate skill as a technician
and his limitless imagination earned
him the title of the 'Wizard of
Nancy.'*

1

Bridging The Centuries

(LEFT) *A wonderfully exuberant example of Bohemian glass consisting of vase and pedestal in amber coloured glass with ornate white and gold decoration by the firm J. & L. Lobmeyr.*

In Great Britain, the 19th century was plagued with confusion and intellectual uncertainty: the Greek, the Etruscan, the medieval, the Tudor and the Gothic all vied for prominence as the dominant stylistic revival. This antique pastiche reached a crescendo by the middle decades and created a crisis of confidence with far-reaching implications.

The Great Exhibition of 1851, held in the purpose-built Crystal Palace in London's Hyde Park, afforded the necessary cathartic action and signalled a turning point in the history of design. It not only provided a most wonderful shop-window display of all that was vacuous and ostentatious about the 19th century, but also represented the swan song of that very culture it was intended to promote. Such a complex state of affairs is worthy of considerable study and explanation but to do this we must look initially to the influence of the Industrial Revolution.

The birthplace of much that powered the Industrial Revolution was Great Britain, which boasted a wealth of talented engineers and inventors who made contributions to science and technology that shaped the modern world. The birth of the Machine Age cast a long shadow over the countryside, while the attraction of steady jobs in the newly created mills and factories drained the land of people and resources. The glass industry, however, was slow to adopt the methods of mass-production and mechanization, and it was not until the late 1880s that this was achieved on any large scale.

If we look at the context within which such radical changes were being proposed, we discover an industry whose working methods had changed little in over 2,000 years. Glass production in the 1880s, although it encompassed a broad spectrum of forms and techniques, was still based on the traditional method of 'design by making'. This relied on the skilled handling of the experienced craftsman and his innate knowledge of the material itself. Steeped in the craft's tradition, the glassblower would probably have learned his art after a long apprenticeship under the guidance of his father, who would probably in turn have learned it from his father.

The general economic slump of the 1830s and 1840s, however, had shaken the industry and forced a reaction. The role of the machine in increasing profits had to be reassessed, as had that of design itself. Good design was seen as paramount if the country was to maintain its share of what was becoming an increasingly competitive world market.

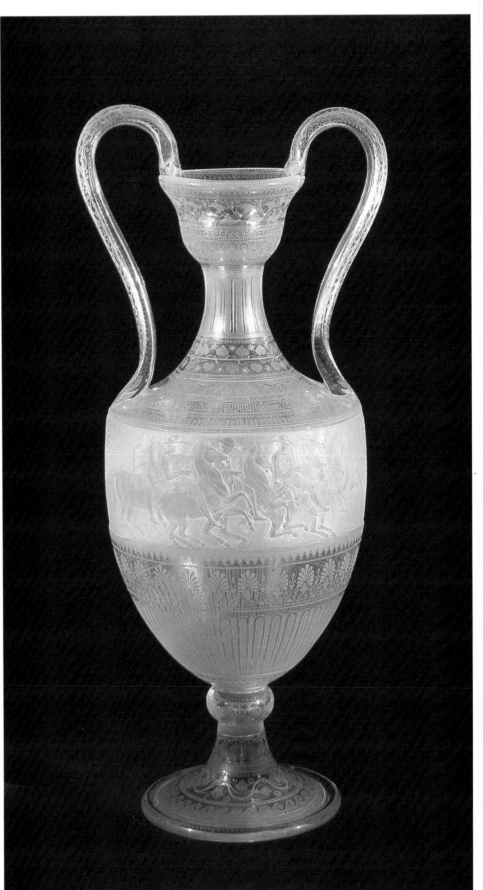

(LEFT) *A colourful scene outside the Crystal Palace which housed the Great Exhibition of 1851; more than 50% of the acres of exhibition space was taken up by British manufacturers. The amazing speed with which the Palace was constructed – nine months – captured the public imagination. Such speed of construction was only made possible by the use of prefabricated mass-produced units.*

(RIGHT) *The Elgin Vase, completed in 1873 by John Northwood, echoed the Victorian vogue for the Neo-classical in art, architecture and design.*

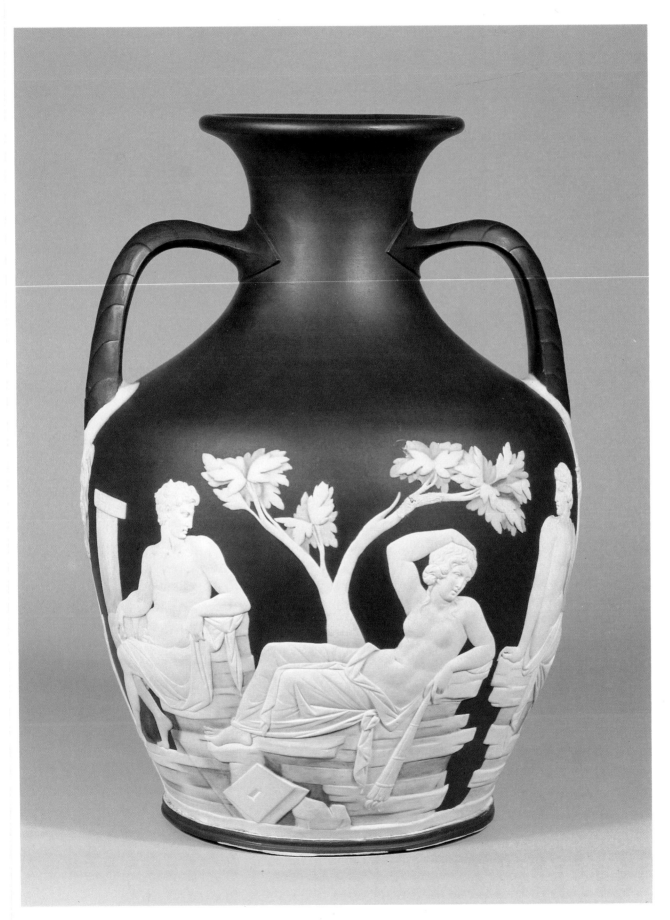

(LEFT) *The sublime vision of recumbent antiquity as portrayed in the famous Portland Vase. This copy dates from c.1790 and was made in unglazed black stoneware at the Wedgwood factory at Etruria.*

(RIGHT) *Mosque Lamp (c.1870) by Joseph Brocard in clear and blue-tinted glass with a complex layering of several geometric patterns which overlap and intermesh (height 12½in/317mm).*

But Britain was not alone in this perilous financial predicament: all of the developed countries recognized the important part played by design in securing exports and all strove to express their particular national identity through the design of their products. On the Continent, for example, the glass-works of Germany and Bohemia were popularizing the Biedermeier style of furniture, but in glass it was characterized by very detailed engraved designs, often with hand-coloured enamel painting. A thin layer of either ruby-, amethyst- or yellow-coloured glass was flashed on top of the clear glass and then cut away to highlight the engraved decoration which lay just below the surface.

In Great Britain, the home market had been temporarily swamped with inexpensive cameo copies which exploited the commercial benefits of acid-etching. Not long after, the cut crystal so beloved by the general public regained its earlier popularity. At the same time the introduction of steam power allowed rows of cutting lathes to be run off one machine, and this important development meant a commensurate drop in production costs. Many classic Georgian designs were hurriedly revived or reinterpreted, but the increasing programme of mechanization produced primarily a surfeit of uninspired, monotonously mitred cross-hatching which required little or no skill from the glass-cutter.

Antique passions

The most influential figure at the time was John Northwood (1836–1902), who worked at Stourbridge, near Birmingham. Northwood was responsible for what is arguably the most influential piece of 19th-century glass: the Portland Vase.

Born at the foot of Glass Hill in a small village near Stourbridge, Northwood epitomized the Victorian ideals of hard work and learned dedication. His technical achievements included the development of a geometrical etching machine in 1865 which could trace simple patterns into a thin layer of wax which coated the glass. Immersed in an acid bath, the incised pattern was revealed. Such a simple technique dispensed with the need for expensive wheel-engraving by hand and allowed, for the first time, thin, delicate glass to be highly decorated.

His greatest contribution to the history of glass, however, must be as a glassmaker, not a manufacturer. His most celebrated work reflects the High Victorian passion for the classical splendours of Antiquity typified by the stolen architectural spoils of Lord Elgin, then recently unveiled at the British Museum in London. The lithe forms of the Athenian horsemen comprising the Parthenon frieze provided the ideal model.

The first of these was the influential Elgin Vase, which involved some nine years of work before its completion in 1873. It generated considerable interest, but its popular success was overshadowed by the Portland Vase of 1876. This was the first successful true copy of the famous Roman vase, dating from the 1st century BC, which was also housed in the British Museum. Made from cobalt-blue glass with a white casing, the work was finished after four years of painstaking engraving by Northwood. The Portland Vase met with enormous public acclaim and was quickly followed by the Milton Vase in 1878 and the the Pegasus Vase in 1882, both decorated in a similar neo-Classical vein.

At around the same time on the Continent, a Frenchman called Joseph Brocard (*fl.* 1867–90) met with similar success in his reinterpretation of not Classical but Islamic themes. His work reflected the strong cultural and political connections between France and the Muslim countries of Northern Africa. Syrian mosque lamps from the 13th and 14th centuries were meticulously copied and used as a source material for floral and geometric decorative patterns. Some pieces by Brocard were later mistaken for the true originals.

The work of such men was widely publicized through numerous magazines and periodicals, very often with pictures and diagrams. This rapid and wide dispersal of

(RIGHT) *Engraving (c.1740) depicting the Verrière or* Glassmacherin *bedecked with a selection of glass utensils.*

ideas, combined with the increasing mechanization of the glass industry, led to a growing tendency towards a greater proliferation of available products, thanks to expanding demand.

The market for such products had burgeoned with the rise of the lower middle class and those aspiring to be the new bourgeoisie. Most of the major glass manufacturers had already adopted new working methods based on the concept of the division of labour as pioneered by Josiah Wedgwood (1730–95) at his Etruria pottery in Staffordshire in the late 18th century. The systematic use of machinery was considered essential to reduce manufactur-

ing costs and thus ensure the necessary increase in profits. Such a move meant that by the end of the 19th century the process of design was finally and irrevocably wrested away from the artist-craftsman and given over to the draughtsman. Instead of the traditional inter-dependence of process and form, the creative impulse was shackled to the drawing board. Instead of the traditional sequence of manipulation and modification during the making, the creative, and final, decisions over form and decoration were made in two dimensions, on paper, often by people with little or no glassblowing experience rather than by the craftsmen themselves.

(LEFT) *Coupled with the lady on the opposite page is the* Verrier *or* Glassmacher, *sporting a complementary selection of glass vessels and utensils.*

The glass industry was now beginning to doubt its traditional role and began to buckle somewhat under an increasingly complex matrix of forces. Thus as the volume of sales increased, so did the degree of choice: but as the variety of glass products expanded, so did the importance of design. As the uniformity of appearance grew, so did the need to express individuality, and artist-craftsmen strove to maintain their creative integrity.

These factors, coupled with the realization that foreign trade was not only profitable but indeed essential to the economic well-being of a country, gave rise to a common desire to embody nationalistic ideas vis-à-vis design. This patriotic upsurge in turn gave rise to a series of expansive national and international expositions. Such events became a regular feature of the period and afforded the particular host nation a carefully orchestrated opportunity to swell national pride and see off any foreign competition at the same time.

The first of such events in Great Britain was the Birmingham Exhibition of 1849. It focused attention on the coloured and pressed glass of Stourbridge and neighbouring factories. Each piece was individually catalogued and discussed at length in the various papers and journals of the day. The conflicting arguments generated a lively forum for public debate which again focused attention on the vexed question of style.

One of the main protagonists in this debate was Augustus Welby Northmore Pugin (1812–52). He was the principal designer of the Houses of Parliament, along with the architect Sir Charles Barry, and almost single-handedly initiated the nostalgic Gothic Revival of the 1840s. Pugin was a devout Catholic (he converted to the religion in 1834) and fervently believed that the Gothic was morally the only proper embodiment of nationhood. He therefore argued vehemently for the adoption of Gothic forms, in both art and design.

Pugin was without doubt the most outspoken and forthright critic of his day. His writings possessed a passion which stuck a chord with a small but influential circle of men, some of whom were to be closely involved with the planning of the Great Exhibition of 1851. They echoed his lament about falling standards in design and shared his deep mistrust of mechanization and the changes it would bring. As early as 1835, the architect CR Cockerell had warned that'. . . the attempt to supersede the work of the mind and hand by mechanical process for the sake of economy will always have the effect of degrading and ultimately ruining art.'

THE BOHEMIAN LEGACY

The Kulm Goblet (c.1835–50) was one of three known goblets made to commemorate the dedication of a monument to the Battle of Kulm (1813) which marked an important victory in the Napoleonic War, (height 10½in/256mm).

Among all the countries that once belonged to the Holy Roman Empire of German Nations, Bohemia has for centuries past produced the most outstanding items of glass. The skills of the Bohemian glass cutter were refined during the 17th and 18th centuries before reaching their zenith between the years 1825–60. Glass was often stained red, yellow or ultramarine before being wheel-cut and then engraved, enamelled, gilded or all three. The ingenuity of the Bohemian glass cutter knew no bounds and the incised decoration became more and more elaborate.

(LEFT) *A selection of late 19th-century glassware, mostly from North America, which would have saddened men such as Morris and Ruskin because it attempted to mimic porcelain and deny the inherent characteristics of the material.*

The unity of mankind

Such doubts, however, were not shared by Prince Albert, who was elected President of the Royal Society of Arts in 1848. His enlightened patronage and earnest support for both art and industry made him well-qualified for his new role. It was his commitment and immense personal energy that made the Great Exhibition of 1851 possible at all. He enthused 'we are living in a period of most wonderful transition which tends rapidly to the accomplishment of that great end to which indeed all of history points, the realization of the unity of mankind.'

His enthusiasm was endemic and reflected in the colossal scale of the final project. Everything about the Great Exhibition was enormous: the attendance figures, the number of products on display and particularly the size of the Exhibition Hall itself, which measured some 1,800 feet (549 metres) in length by 140 feet (43 metres) in height.

The significance of glass in such a bold venture was reflected in the very name and composition of the Exhibition building: the Crystal Palace. This breathtaking piece of engineering combined glass, iron and wood in what was the most celebrated fusion between art and industry that had ever been undertaken. Derived from an idea hurriedly sketched out on the back of an envelope, the designer, Joseph Paxton, had only a matter of months to design, fabricate and erect this enormous structure in London's Hyde Park. His ambitious scheme necessitated the manufacture of over a million square feet of glass, a task which fell to the Chance Brothers of Smethwick, near Birmingham.

The Great Exhibition, or the Exhibition of the Industry of All Nations, as it was officially designated, brought together for the first time all the major manufacturing industries from around the world. Most of the leading glasshouses were well represented and the competition to carry off some of the judges' medals was intense. The opportunity to exhange, to compare or even just to plagiarize ideas proved a considerable stimulus to the already present rivalry between competing firms.

The Exhibition attracted over six million visitors during its brief five-month duration and generated a heated debate among an increasingly discerning and cosmopolitan general public. Here, as with the earlier exhibition in Birmingham, a detailed catalogue ensured the prolongation of the debate long after the Exhibition closed.

The diverse range of work on display presented a veritable cornucopia from around the world. Simple hand-made goods from the undeveloped edges of the Empire were laid out next to the most extravagant machine-made work, overburdened with superfluous ornamentation. Even the official report points out that '. . . wherever ornament is wholly effected by machinery, it is certainly the most degraded in style and execution; and the best workmanship and the best taste are to be found in those manufacturers . . . wherin handicraft is entirely or partially the means of producing the ornament.'

Much of the glass on display, however, was either derivative and/or uninspired. Shelf after shelf was stacked with vast quantities of cut crystal to satisfy an ever-expanding domestic market. Social aspirations wer such that any proper table service had to contain a different glass for each particular beverage, be it white wine, red wine, champagne, brandy, punch, ale, porter, water and so on, yet each glass had to be identical in its ornamentation.

Most of the Engish crystal was in clear leaded glass, heavily cut in diamond or mitred patterns, and was singled out for praise in the official catalogue. Cut crystal was sited as the epitome of the glassmakers' art and one firm,

Apsley and Co, boasted that 'the essential . . . qualities of good glass are its near resemblance to real crystal in its brilliant, refractive and colourless transparency. In all respects, the productions of the British glass-houses are at present unrivalled.'

Such patriotic modesty was also subtly encapsulated by the Grand Crystal Fountain. Nearly 20 feet (just over six metres) tall, the fountain dominated the transept of the main nave and was seen as the fulcrum for the entire exhibition. Manufactured by F and C Osler, of Birmingham, a company specializing in large theatrical glass objects, its massive scale aptly reflected the 19th-century desire for grandeur expressed by sheer size.

This elaborate composite structure was carried by iron supports '. . . so completely embedded in the glass shafts as to be invisible and in no way interfering with the purity and crystalline effect of the whole object'. The polished lead glass was highly decorated with deep prismatic cutting to enhance its light refracting qualities, which combined with the cascading jets of water to produce a sparkling sculpture of diamond-like brilliance. Its prominent location and scale were such as to convince any doubting visitor that English crystal was indeed unrivalled in the world.

(RIGHT) *A glass plaque bearing the rather grandiose title of 'The Immortality of the Arts' (1887); it was made at Brierly Hill by Stevens & Williams and signed by Frederick Carder. The plaque combines opaque white glass over translucent amber glass which was then acid-dipped and cameo-carved to reveal the detail; (diameter 13in/330mm).*

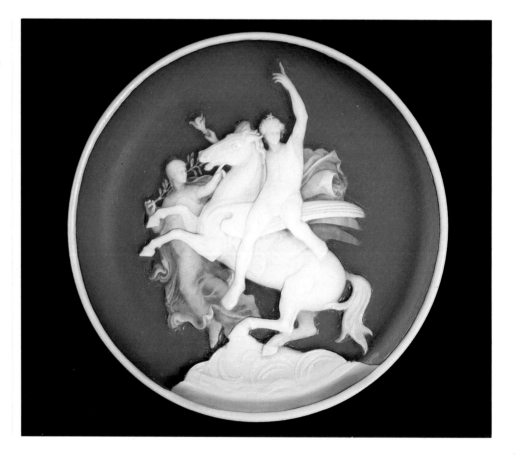

Such vacuous vulgarity was not to everyone's taste, of course, and in the official report Richard Redgrave warned that when '. . . the ornament so largely prevails to the exclusion of the useful . . . it is apt to sicken us of decoration and lead us to admire those objects of absolute utility, where use is so paramount that ornament is repudiated and fitness of purpose being the end sought, a noble simplicity is the result'. This dichotomy between what was written and what was exhibited was a deliberate attempt by Redgrave and some of the organizers to educate and awaken the public to what they felt to be the degenerate deterioration of design standards. Henry Cole, the principal organizer, castigated the machine as the primary cause and blamed it for having usurped the craftsman's control over the forms of production.

The significance of the exhibition in the development of Modernism is generally agreed by design historians to be without parallel. Indeed, the repercussions of such an extraordinary event were to echo through to the end of that century and beyond. The Great Exhibition can therefore be seen as truly seminal for both the 19th and 20th centuries; not only did it engender an unbridled outpouring of creativity, much of which was tasteless and pretentious, but it also accelerated the first hesitant moves towards a contemporary theory of design.

(TOP) *An early hand-tinted postcard of the Crystal Palace exhibition complex after its move from the original site in London's Hyde Park to Sydenham, where it was so tragically destroyed by fire some years later.*

(ABOVE) *Some six million visitors from every nation crowded into the Great Exhibition of 1851 during its five month duration. The overwhelming success of the exhibition proved to have far-reaching implications.*

(BELOW) *In Great Britain, the Birmingham Exhibition of 1849 was the first of many subsequent international expositions. The resultant cornucopia of bad taste and over-elaboration often suffocated both design and common sense.*

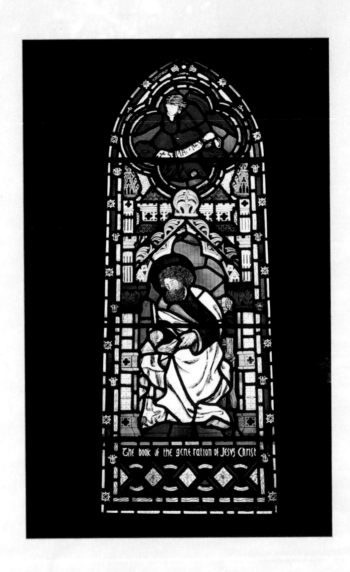

2

Arts & Crafts and the Aesthetic Movement

The image of St Matthew transcribing the first gospel of the New Testament by Morris & Company, 1862; Lady Chapel, Christchurch, London.

In the vanguard of the somewhat hesitant movement towards a contemporary theory of design were two English theorists, John Ruskin (1819–1900) and William Morris (1834–96). Their work and writings sprang from a common belief in the sanctity of nature, the value of the individual and the importance of the hand-crafted object. Their approach to everything was underpinned by a reasoned, yet heartfelt philosophy of design, not simply an agglomeration of decorative motifs so typical of much of the 19th century. Instead, they lived by the tenet that all things should be 'fit for a purpose'.

The attitude of the British glass industry, not surprisingly, mirrored that of the general public and treated such puritanical leanings toward functionalism with considerable mistrust. Why should they make do with less when there was so much to possess? Morris's edict – that you should '. . . have nothing in your homes that you do not know to be useful, or believe to be beautiful' – was bordering on the extreme for most people and suggested an all-too-spartan lifestyle. Instead, they preferred to languish in a sea of heavily cut crystal, where every glass was identical and overlaid with opulent ornamentation.

Such polarization provoked a predictably spirited response from Ruskin and Morris. Only two years after the Great Exhibition, Ruskin wrote in his book, *The Stones of Venice,* that 'all cut glass is barbarous, for the cutting conceals its ductility and confuses it with crystal. Also, all very neat, finished and perfect form in glass is barbarous . . .' Instead he called for a greater respect for the material's instrinsic characteristics, and laid particular emphasis on its ductility, the plastic qualities inherent in molten glass. The purity of colour which glass allows was also attractive to Ruskin in an almost abstract sense: 'The purest and most thoughtful minds are those which love colour the most.'

The question of whether glass should be seen as a plastic or a glyptic art, where it is incised or carved like semiprecious stone, is one that recurs repeatedly throughout the history of glass. The origins of such a debate are vague, but may well spring from the original Greek derivation of the word 'glass', meaning 'poured stone'. For Ruskin such tenuous arguments were irrelevant. His approach was straightforward and dogmatic: 'I believe the right question to ask, respecting all ornament, is simply this: was it done with enjoyment, was the carver happy when he was about it?'

Commercial tyranny

Ruskin's revulsion at the excesses of the 19th century was such that he believed the only answer was to completely abandon the previous 150 years of material progress. He argued that the only redemption from the unending drudgery of the factory sweatshop was a return to medieval social values and the ancient traditions of handicrafts. He believed that: 'You must make either a tool of the creature or a man of him, you cannot make both. Men were not intended to work with the accuracy of tools, to be precise and perfect in all their actions. If you will have that precision out of them, and make their fingers measure degrees like cog-wheels, and their arms strike curves like compasses, you must unhumanise them.'

In contrast with Ruskin's recidivist pessimism, Morris offered what was in effect an early precursor of modern-day socialism. He called for a more caring society, and foresaw a more optimistic vision of a world protected from the uncaring actions of the capitalists by the egalitarian bounds of brotherhood and equality. For Morris, the machine was the willing lackey of the greedy businessman sacrificing design quality for more monetary gain.

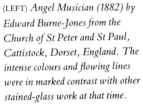

He insisted that 'It is not this or that tangible steel and brass machine which we want to get rid of, but the great intangible machine of commercial tyranny which oppresses the lives of all of us.' Morris challenged the glass industry to break away from mechanization and in doing so unburden the inherent creativity of the individual craftsman. Thus, his particular personality, could influence his work, resulting in something that was unique.

As a practical affirmation of his philosophical beliefs, Morris commissioned his friend and former colleague Philip Webb (1831–1915) to design a new home for his wife and himself. Situated at Bexleyheath in Kent, the Red House, as it was known, was completed in 1859. It provided an opportune testing ground for the Arts and Crafts ideal. For Morris this was no mere self-indulgent whim but a utopian blueprint for what was possible for not only the wealthy, but for everyone. Intended as a protest against the shallowness of contemporary industrial design, the Red House afforded Morris and his like-minded colleagues a unique opportunity to explore every aspect of the domestic interior from patterned wallpaper to kitchen chairs.

(LEFT) Angel Musician (1882) by Edward Burne-Jones from the Church of St Peter and St Paul, Cattistock, Dorset, England. The intense colours and flowing lines were in marked contrast with other stained-glass work at that time.

(BELOW) Two panels depicting the Flight into Egypt by Edward Burne-Jones for Morris & Company (1862) at St Michael's Church, Brighton, England.

The success of this venture was such that in 1861 Morris finally abandoned his youthful ambition of becoming a painter, and instead devoted his efforts to setting up a company to promote, manufacture and sell Arts and Crafts products to the general public. Operating under the rather grandiose title of Morris, Marshall, Faulkner and Company, Fine Art Workmen in Painting, Carving and Furniture and Metals, they hoped not only to educate a public satiated with ornamentation, but also to reform the means of production by arguing that to '. . . give people pleasure in the things they must perforce *use*, that is one great office of decoration; to give people pleasure in the things they must perforce *make*, that is the other use of it.'

In glass, attention was focused primarily on ecclesiastical stained-glass windows. Several noteworthy commissions were completed, usually in conjunction with the artist Edward Burne-Jones (1833–98). Glassware was on the whole largely ignored by Morris & Co, except for one notable exception. This was the range of chunky glass tumblers manufactured by Whitefriars in 1860 (later reissued in 1903), which were designed by Philip Webb. As with his architecture, Webb looked first to traditional forms as a basis, in this instance to the domestic furnishings of 17th-century Holland as portrayed in the still-life paintings of Jan van Eyck and his contemporaries. The lack of ornament and distinctive shape of the tumblers

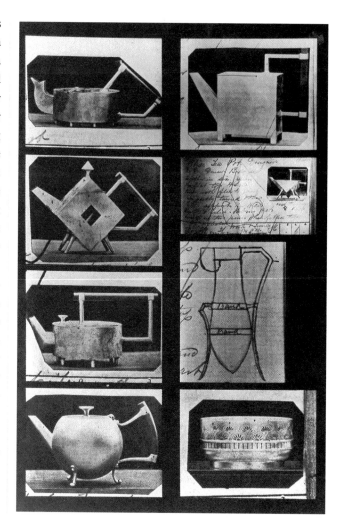

(ABOVE) *This remarkable collection of prototype designs were executed by Christopher Dresser for the Sheffield firm of James Dixon and Sons Ltd. They date from 1879 and therefore precede the prismatic forms of the cubist revolution by over 30 years.*

(LEFT) Still Life with Gun, *Pieter van Steenwyck; it was paintings such as this 17th-century Dutch* vanitas, *depicting simple, unadorned glassware, which inspired Philip Webb to design tumblers with the same lack of ornament as early as 1860.*

(RIGHT) *Antonio Salviati was the driving force behind the resurgence of the Venetian glass industry. This bowl (1879) demonstrates his technical flair in weaving multi-coloured glass with silver foil (height 7in/173mm)*

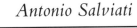

set them apart from any equivalent Victorian glassware. The stripping down of unneccesary frills suggests a time-less, almost puritanical quality which is derived explicitly from their purpose. It is this emphasis on functionalism which begs their classification as modern; a modernity which predates the 20th century's obsession with the functional by some considerable time.

At around the same time, another exhibition opened which was to prove highly influential. Organized by the Royal Society of Art, 'The Art and Architecture of the Ancient and Medieval Eras' featured not only several pieces of Islamic glass from the 14th century, but also many fine examples of early Venetian work from the Felix Slade Collection. Such distinctive pieces, and their attendant working conditions, personified all that Ruskin and Morris aspired to in their utopian model. Their passion for Venetian forms of glassmaking was, for once, widely shared by the public and reflected in the haste with which the museums endeavoured to expand their antique glass collections.

Antonio Salviati

This fashion for antique glass of such individual and delicate form prompted a serious revival in the ancient art of glassmaking on the island of Murano in the Venetian lagoon, the traditional home of Italian glassmaking. The leading figure in this resurgence was Antonio Salviati (1816–90), who achieved not only commercial success, but also considerable critical acclaim. Salviati's thriving workshop exploited both the indigenous skills of local craftsmen and the labour-saving advantages of machine production. Such an inspired coupling was essential if he was to rework intricate 16th-century forms and the re-sultant pieces were to remain affordable to Europe's wealthier households. Many of the ancient techniques, however, had been lost and had to be studiously re-searched and relearned – for example, the production of *latticino* glass, in which clear glass is embedded with thin strands of coloured glass in flowing patterns.

(ABOVE) *Three fine examples of turn-of-the century British glassware by Stevens & Williams. They are, from left to right, a silveria vase, a moss agate vase and a silvered and cameo glass vase.*

Salviati produced a wide range of items which were usually highly decorated and at times prohibitively expensive. Aimed primarily at the newly wealthy middle classes, such exuberant pieces were intended to reflect the social aspirations of the purchaser (the consumer), and as such met with great popular success throughout Europe. In England, his position was assured when, in 1868, a showroom was opened in London's Regent Street and his work was then able to reach an even wider public than before.

The elegant forms and fragile beauty of Venetian glass were quickly assimilated by several of the English glass manufacturers. John Northwood, for example, who in 1881 was artistic director and production manager at Stevens and Williams, pioneered a range of glassware – known as Anglo-Venetian – which displayed considerable technical manipulation and an understanding of Venetian forms. There was also Harry Powell (*fl.* 1880s–1910s), who in 1875 was appointed principal director and designer at the Whitefriars Glass Works in London. He produced a range of table service in the Venetian manner made

(RIGHT) *Flower bowl (c.1904) in green glass by James Powell & Sons of Whitefriars. The pewter base was probably designed by Archibald Knox for the London department store of Liberty.*

from subtly coloured green soda glass which was in production right up to about 1910. Powell's inventive re-interpretation of the Venetian style rose above most such work, which often simply plagiarized recognizable motifs without contributing anything new to the genre. His work also included thinly blown glass vessels, such as jugs, goblets and decanters in a tinted opalescent glass which paid homage to William Morris's argument that glass should contain tiny specks and faint streaks because '. . . these things make the form visible'.

The English contribution

Few of Morris's ideas filtered into the mainstream of English culture at the time. The vast majority marginalized him as a misguided ascetic, while others simply dismissed him as a romantic. It is only now, with the benefit of a historical perspective, that many people realize how important his ideas were in the development of 20th-century design. Morris's vision of a proto-socialist Utopia where the drudgery of long hours spent toiling over machines would be banished and men would instead practice an honest craft was, of course, fundamentally flawed. His egalitarian dream of bringing beauty within

the reach of everyman was impossible because everything had to be hand-made. The costs of such objects were therefore out of the reach of the very people he had hoped to influence. Although aware of this paradox towards the end of his life, he nevertheless held true to his belief that '. . . machines can do everything – except make great works of art', and in the book, *Art of the People*, he wrote 'Real art is the expression by man of his pleasure in labour. I do not believe he can be happy in his labour without expressing that happiness; and especially is this so when he is at work on anything in which he especially excels.'

Morris's death in October 1896 marked the end of England's prominent position within the history of design. Afterwards attention would in general be concentrated on the work of a handful of avant-garde Europeans and Americans. The prosperous Victorian middle classes, whom Morris had despised as the '. . . enemies of beauty and slaves of necessity', felt no great loss at his demise. His work, however, was not completely without recognition, and his example proved an inspiration to several talented young designers at the time.

One such young man was Charles Robert Ashbee (1863–1942), who might be labelled the archetypal English eccentric. He founded the Guild and School of Handicraft,

(LEFT) *Centrepiece designed by Harry Powell in 1903 for James Powell & Sons of Whitefriars; the design reflects the twin influences of the English Arts and Crafts Movement and the Continental Art Nouveau Movement.*

(LEFT) *The immense popularity of Venetian glass spurred several English firms, including James Powell & Sons of Whitefriars, to develop their own individual brand of Anglo-Venetian glass.*

which evolved from a reading class he had chaired on Ruskin in London's East End district. Here he gathered together a collection of enthusiastic but unskilled working men to develop their potential as individual craftsmen. In 1902, the Guild moved far from the corrupting influence of the metropolis to the sleepy Cotswold village of Chipping Campden, where several workshops were set up. Organized as a working cooperative to administer the day-to-day running of the Guild and maintain some financial stability, they explored an extensive range of disciplines, including the making of jewellery, furniture, leatherwork and some glass.

What little work they did produce in glass was simple but modest, and sometimes betrayed a slight tendency towards the sweeping curves of the Art Nouveau style. Inspiration was again historical, and the basic form was usually copied from medieval sources, though often adorned with precious stones. Although the Guild collapsed not long after its move to the countryside in 1908, due to financial difficulties, the concept of a multi-disciplinary, non-hierarchical working community offered a valuable model for similar ventures which were to develop later in Vienna and Darmstadt. These in turn gave rise to the founding of the Bauhaus school in the Weimar

Republic (which will be discussed in a subsequent chapter).

Ashbee had been a one-time associate of Morris and, although eager to adopt the high moral principles of the Arts and Crafts Movement, he was not prepared to be castigated as an intellectual Luddite as both Morris and Ruskin had been in their time. He may have viewed the relentless tide of mechanization with concern, but refused to dismiss it out of hand. His more tolerant attitude to the machine is succinctly expressed in his book, *Craftsmanship in Competitive Industry*, which was published in 1908. In this he argued:

What I seek to show is that this Arts and Crafts movement, which began with the earnestness of the Pre-Raphaelite Painters, the prophetic enthusiasm of Ruskin and the titanic energy of Morris is not what the public has thought it to be, or is seeking to make it: a nursery for luxuries, a hothouse for the production of mere trivialities and useless things for the rich. It is a movement for the stamping out of such things by sound production on the one hand, and the inevitable regulation of machine production and cheap labour on the other.

'Stile Liberty'

Like Morris before him, Ashbee used the firm of James Powell & Sons for any work in glass. The company operated under the title of the Whitefriars Glass Factory and was probably the most forward-looking of any of the English glasshouses. Whitefriars also played a part in the success of the famous London department store, Liberty's, which was to prove so influential in developing a contemporary aesthetic.

The entrepreneurial flair of Liberty's founder, Arthur Lasenby Liberty (1843–1917), was to play a significant role in the development of modern design within both Great Britain and, to a lesser extent, on the continent (in Italy, for instance, the term 'Stile Liberty' was adopted to represent the Italians' particularly floral and baroque version of Art Nouveau). His enlightened policy of utilizing mechanical production techniques to reduce manufacturing costs, yet employing the most talented designers of the day, allowed the ordinary man, for the first time, the opportunity to buy excellence in design. The ethical doctrines of Morris's philosophy were abandoned for a more pragmatic approach to the design of consumer objects for the mass market.

(LEFT) *A footed bowl of clear glass decorated in a geometric pattern in vivid colours with gilded outlines. It was manufactured at the Bachmetor Glassworks, near St. Petersburg in Russia, c.1880 and was probably finished at home by an experienced apprentice; (height 9½in/230mm).*

(ABOVE) *Clear glass vase enamelled by de Lorm showing a mythical dragon in vibrant colours and*

manufactured at the Royal Dutch Glass Works, Leerdam, c.1920; (height 6½in/152mm)

(FAR RIGHT) *One of a series of elegant decanters designed in glass and pewter by Archibald Knox, c.1903, for the London department store of Liberty. The green glass vessel was made by James Powell & Sons of Whitefriars; (height 11¾in/292mm).*

The Liberty store was first opened in 1875 in London's Regent Street, and provided a sound commercial base for several of Britain's most important designers from the early part of the 20th century. The roll-call includes men such as CFA Voysey and Walter Crane, who specialized in the design of wallpapers and fabrics; George Walton and EW Godwin, who dealt with furniture and couture, respectively; and Christopher Dresser (1834–1904) and Archibald Knox (1864–1933), who designed glass and metalwork. The extraordinary output of Christopher Dresser will be discussed in Chapter Five, but Archibald Knox was also a designer of considerable merit.

Knox was the key figure in developing a distinctive style for the store, particularly with his very popular range of Celtic-inspired designs, known as 'Cymric' and

'Tudric'. The popular success of such pieces was due partly to Liberty's reputation for quality craftsmanship, but the main credit must be given to the originality of the designer. Knox's work possessed a purity of form which was in stark contrast to the decadent fussiness of other contemporary Victorian design. The refined quality of such ornamentation was further enhanced by his skilful use of localized decoration, often with semiprecious stones.

Knox's work for Liberty, along with that of every other designer, was anonymous. This policy of anonymity was a subtle ploy to promote the name of the store, not that of any individual designer. The cult of personality was thus neatly avoided, but Liberty was not so successful in overcoming the irreconcilable polarities of mechanical production with social responsibility, as conceived in the original Arts and Crafts ideal. On this matter there lay an unbridgeable chasm between the public-spirited intentions of Morris and the financial pragmaticism of Liberty.

The principal difference between Morris and Liberty was that the latter was a businessman, not a visionary. He readily accepted the inevitable truth that the machine could generate both wealth and misery in equal measure. However, he exploited the benefits it could offer by way of reducing production costs and instead allowed his designers the freedom to experiment with bold new shapes and patterns. He was happy to commission, foster, encourage, retail and publicize such work because it sold. However, he had no true critical understanding of the work of men such as Dresser and Knox. He wrongly believed them to be working in a historicist style, when in fact their output was closer in spirit to the burgeoning Art Nouveau. Liberty mistrusted the meteoric rise in Europe of this movement and dismissed it as that '. . . fantastic motif which pleases our Continental friends to worship as *l'art nouveau*'

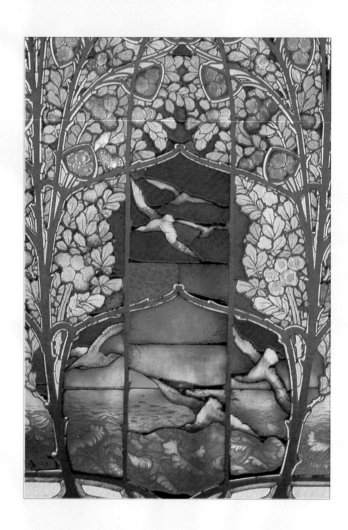

3

Art Nouveau and the Poetic

Stained-glass window by Jacques Gruber for a medical school in Nancy, France. Gruber was Professor of Decorative Arts in the city, at the Ecole des Beaux-Arts. He was part of the renaissance of the glass industry in Nancy, headed by Gallé and the Daum brothers, and showed the same concern for opacity, colour and relief, using acid to eat away layers of glass to reveal hidden colour or powdered enamel fused onto the surface in the furnace to create a glowing, opaque finish.

The mistrust of the English for the energetic new movement called Art Nouveau was a fine example of the island nation's celebrated puritanical and, at times, prudish character. The sweeping 'decadence' and heightened exuberance of Art Nouveau made the English uneasy, while the clarion call of the aesthetic, 'Art for Art's sake', was considered both improper and vain. Such youthful impropriety was inevitably destined to burn itself out after only a few years, but this remarkable, if transitory, movement provided the necessary and final transition between the moribund historicism of the 19th century and the Modern Movement of the 20th century.

The history of Art Nouveau, which the English artist Walter Crane dismissed as a 'strange disease', presents a vivid portrait of fin-de-siecle Europe. That sense of excitement and pre-World War I innocence imbued the arts with a new-found vibrancy and purpose. This new mood touched every sphere within the arts and can be seen in the poetry of Rainer Maria Rilke, the illustrations of Aubrey Beardsley, the music of Richard Strauss, the paintings of Henri de Toulouse-Lautrec, the architecture of Victor Horta and the chairs of Henry van de Velde.

The common thread that links these separate figures was a belief in man's subjugated role within the larger natural world. They believed that only through Nature could one find truth in Art. She was therefore minutely dissected as the ultimate source book for 'great Art' which, in turn, could only be found in the transformation of the natural object.

The curve

For most people this fascination for Nature was embodied in the movement's characteristic visual motif: the long and sinuous extended curve. As a recognizable leitmotif, this arabesque line works admirably well but it belies the true intellectual depth of thought behind the aspirations of Art Nouveau. The initial ideas which gave rise to the movement belong to the French writer and architect Eugène Emmanuel Viollet-le-Duc (1814–79). He championed the call for the development of a contemporary new style to act as a clean break from the continual regurgitation of past historical themes. In pursuit of this he also demanded that materials be used honestly. He

(RIGHT) *Twinned vases by Emile Gallé; (height 20in/508mm).*

(RIGHT) *Gallé realized the potential of the recently invented incandescent light bulb and created a series of glass table lamps to exploit Edison's new discovery; (height 27in/67mm).*

vehemently opposed the teachings of the omnipotent Ecole des Beaux-Arts, which propagated the common practice of constructing enormous edifices, apparently hewn out of solid stone but in reality carried by a slender supporting iron frame which was then cloaked within a thin veneer of real stone. Viollet-le-Duc argued that such trickery was not only dishonest but also unsettling to the human psyche.

In discussing the sources of Art Nouveau, it should be remembered that this was also the era of great strides in anthropology, the science of man, and psychology, the science of the mind. The writings of Sigmund Freud, who in 1900 published his book, *The Interpretation of Dreams*, both shocked and fascinated European intellectuals. His exploration of psychological techniques to unlock the hidden meanings of dreams and apparitions was highly influential in increasing the designer's awareness of how outside factors influenced the human conscious-

ness and lent added credence to the new tendencies within design itself.

Many felt that the sudden surge of industrialization and the resulting flood of mechanically produced goods had to be redressed by a more considered approach. The importance of one's immediate environment and surrounding objects had become a common concern; the principal worry was what effects, if any, machine-made objects might have on the human psyche.

Advocates of Art Nouveau did not intend to deny the benefits of the machine, as exponents of the Arts and Crafts Movement had, but simply wanted to arrest any slide into soul-less mechanized repetition. To achieve this they strove to develop a mutually beneficial partnership between the creative inner soul and the new technological advances. In so doing they hoped to maximize the potential of both forces and overcome possible conflicts.

(OPPOSITE) *Gallé's acute observation of natural form is evident in all his work. He quickly began to experiment with different techniques to control degrees of colour and translucency, using acid baths to oxidize pieces, moulding to achieve relief effects, or embedding further elements within the glass, such as metal leaf, gold dust or enamel.*

(RIGHT) *This overlay vase demonstrates Gallé's 'carved hardstone' method; (height 5½in/ 132mm).*

An obvious extension of this argument was to unite the previously separate activities of fine art and industrial art. This symbiotic coexistence is well demonstrated by the work of Emile Gallé, Louis Tiffany and other glass-makers of the time. The inherent characteristics of glass allowed such men the opportunity to probe that nebulous area beyond the strict limits of one's consciousness. Their skill lay in being able to extend our imagination by exploring their own personal interpretations of Nature transformed. The insubstantiality, the malleability and flexibility of glass afforded them the ideal medium in which to exploit the possibilities of the undulating line or the extended curve.

Although primarily a Continental phenomenon, many of the ideas behind Art Nouveau were originally derived from the English Arts and Crafts Movement. Indeed the first work is usually attributed to Arthur Heygate Mackmurdo (1851–1942), who designed an evocative cover for his book on Sir Christopher Wren's city churches, published in 1883. The name 'Art Nouveau' itself was taken from a shop in Paris called 'La Maison de l'Art Nouveau'. The proprietor was a German émigré called Siegfried Bing (1838–1905), who had previously been a dealer in Japanese art in Hamburg before moving to the French capital to set up this bold new venture. Its opening in December 1895 scandalized respectable Parisian society. The work of radical young artists such as Gallé and Tiffany met with both enthusiastic praise and savage criticism in equal measure.

Possibly the most striking feature of this new movement was the speed with which it swept across Europe, ignoring both cultural and political barriers. Within a matter of years it was the predominant national style throughout the Continent, from Spain and Portugal in the west, through to Russia and Czechoslovakia in the east. Its rapid growth, however, was mirrored by its sudden demise. Having developed in the late 1880s, it peaked with the Paris Exposition Universelle of 1900, and had lost its youthful vitality by the time of the Liège Exposition in 1905. Its artistic legacy, however, was both impressive and influential, particularly so in the area of glassmaking, where its reputation rests principally with the work of two men: Emile Gallé (1846–1904) and Louis Comfort Tiffany (1848–1933).

(LEFT) *The work of Gallé is now highly collectable and can command commensurate prices, this Wisteria double-overlay glass table lamp, for example, was valued for auction in 1985 at a figure of $70–90,000.*

(RIGHT) *Delicately shaped rectangular vase by François Eugène Rousseau, bearing the head of a grotesque figure; (width 14½in/360mm).*

GALLÉ

. . . .

'The execution of personal dreams'

Born in Nancy, France, Gallé was the son of a glass-maker from the Lorraine, Charles Gallé-Reinemer, with whom he worked before studying art at Weimar. Gallé not only possessed considerable skill in the traditional techniques of French glassmaking, but was also well experienced in undertaking exact copies of 16th-century German enamelled-glass *Humpen* beakers. His most important early influence, however, was Joseph Brocard. Gallé, like Brocard, made numerous visits to the great museums of London and Paris to make detailed drawings of early Islamic glass as a means of unravelling the complex interlocking patterns which crowd the surface of 14th-century mosque lamps and the like. Like many of his contemporaries, Gallé was excited by the recent 'discovery' by the West of the ancient arts of Japan. The characteristic feature of this Japanese art was its striking juxtaposition of asymmetrical composition with the delicate use of line and colour. Such invention shattered the traditionally accepted standards of the day and gave rise to an insatiable cult for things Japanese, termed 'Japonisme'.

In 1878, at an exhibition of contemporary work organized by the Union Centrale des Arts Décoratifs, which was later to instigate the founding of the Musée des Arts Décoratifs in Paris, Gallé met Eugène Rousseau (1827–91). He was an art dealer-turned-craftsman who had just launched a Japanese-inspired range of glassware. Rousseau was acknowledged as a gifted innovator and had developed several new decorative techniques involving relief-work, inscriptions, gold leaf and tracery crazing.

Rousseau's more daring work stirred Gallé to adopt a more personal, idiosyncratic approach and break away from the restrictive use of historical precedent. He experimented with every possible form of glass, including coloured, opaque, marbled and enamelled overlay. Close control over the production process was required if Gallé was to achieve the subtle changes in translucency or colour necessary to achieve his ambitious vision. This involved the careful study of temperature and chemical composition, which was essential in developing the great variety of techniques he employed – for example, the use of oxidization by acid to give an antique look to glass, or the process of filtering various elements within the layers of glass, such as metal leaf, gold dust or enamel.

He was also skilled in creating a heightened sense of relief either through the use of moulds or by employing acid which could cut away the top layers to reveal the hidden colours beneath. He could therefore build up a delicately modulated surface texture or alternatively a

deeply contoured shape, depending on his inclination or need. His most distinctive technical achievement, however, was the development of marqueterie-sur-verre, in which semifluid layers of glass were laid over the semimolten vessel to create bold, sculptural effects.

Gallé's subject matter reflected his early passions, namely, literature, botany, natural history and the exotic Orient. For him, Nature was the only legitimate source, and he therefore endeavoured to fashion each individual piece into a microcosm of the natural, fluctuating world – a world which, for example, revolved around a butterfly's wing, a drifting water reed or a swaying flower stem. His later work may be seen as either symbolist or impressionist, depending upon the mood of each individual piece, and this ambiguity is well summed up by a contemporary critic who wrote: 'An artist like Gallé makes us think of a quintessential abstraction that attempts to materialize the impalpable and to turn the dream into glass.'

This desire to reveal the workings of the subconscious is prevalent in much of Galle's later work and he himself admitted:

My own work consists above all in the execution of personal dreams: to dress crystal in tender and terrible roles, to compose for it the thoughtful faces of pleasure and tragedy, to assemble all the elements and carefully prepare the effective production of my future projects, to order techniques in the service of preconceived works of art, and to weigh the operational scale of chance with possibilities for success at the time of the decisive operation, once called the masterwork. In other words, in so far as I am capable, from the start, I impose upon it qualities I should like it to have – the material and its colorations, the material and its measures – in order to incarnate my dreams and my design.

His œuvre also included a series known as *verreries parlantes*, or 'talking glass', which contain inscribed quotations from the literary works of his compatriots. These were intended as his tribute to a shared poetic sensibility, and encompassed passages from Rimbaud, Verlaine, Baudelaire and Victor Hugo. The enormous success of these and other such objects obliged him to employ some 300 people to meet the huge demand. This expansion of his work force allowed Gallé to spend

more time on his unique, one-off experimental pieces, while the factory produced copy upon copy of his more conventional vessels.

Despite occupying such a privileged position, Gallé's humanity also extended to the day-to-day conditions of the working man. He was by no means oblivious to the radical changes happening within society and warned of the '. . . age of industrialization with its excessive division of labour, its organized management located in a poisoned and artificial atmosphere, far from the domestic hearth, the family, and the natural environment. The century that is about to end did not have its own popular art, that is to say, no art applied to useful objects and executed spontaneously, joyously by the various artisans of each craft.'

He nevertheless believed that beauty could be offered to the masses and at an affordable price: 'Neither I, nor my workmen, have found it impossible to reconcile cheap production with art.' This socially enlightened attitude was also echoed in the United States by Louis Comfort Tiffany, whose glass factory manufactured an extensive catalogue of beautifully crafted products for the mass market which included cologne bottles, tobacco jars, cigar lighters, marmalade jars, decanters, cruet sets, jewellery boxes and the like.

TIFFANY:

. . . .

An American aesthetic

Tiffany was born into a wealthy New York merchant family and as a young man enjoyed all the privileges of the American nouveau-riche. His father's prosperous department store, Tiffany & Co, afforded him the money to travel extensively across Europe, North Africa and the Middle East. Here he developed a great love for the exotic, and particularly the ancient culture of Islam. He visited numerous mosques and caravanserai, where he would painstakingly measure and then draw the complex interlocking patterns of the ceramic tile-work or timber latticework. This craving for the complexity of Islamic architecture was stirred by the Koranic concept of *horror vacui*, which demanded that all blank surfaces be decorated with some type of pattern, preferably geometric in form. Tiffany was by now an accomplished painter but, having seen the work of Gallé in Paris, he decided to redirect his talents towards the decorative arts and glassmaking in particular.

He opened his first major glassworks in 1893 at Corona on Long Island, New York, and employed an Englishman, Arthur Nash, as chief designer and factory

(FAR LEFT) *This Tiffany vase of opaque glass is typical of the unusual patterning and coloration that were produced under the Favrile banner between 1892 and 1920; (height 10½in/225mm).*

(LEFT) *A selection of glassware from the studios of Louis Comfort Tiffany, including an iridescent glass lily lampshade.*

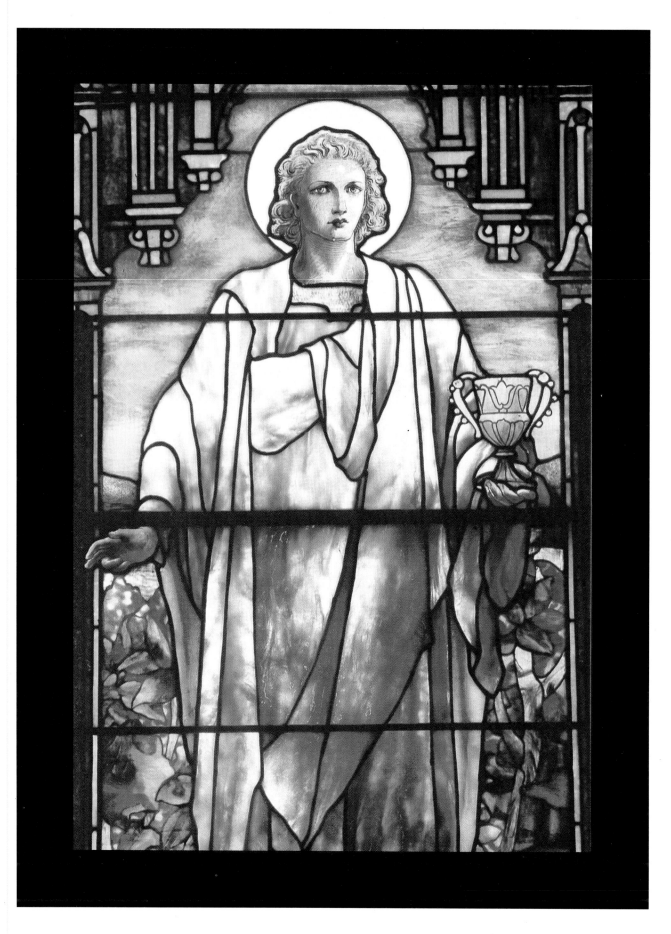

manager. Nash, having served his time with Thomas Webb & Sons of Stourbridge, brought the necessary experience to this talented partnership. They not only enjoyed a long and profitable period together but also played a critical role in developing a contemporary aesthetic in the United States. Tiffany was a man of considerable energy and entrepreneurial flair, and, having abandoned painting, he instead excelled at a varied cross-section of the other arts, including stained glass, mosaics, enamelling, ceramics, furniture and interior design. He is best remembered, however, for his work in glass, and especially the Favrile range of one-off hand-blown art pieces. The term 'favrile' was adapted from the Old English word 'fabrile', meaning 'belonging to a craftsman or his craft'. Tiffany produced several thousand such pieces before his death in 1933: each was individually designed and hand-crafted, each was finished in a distinctive iridescent hue and each was carefully checked by Tiffany himself before leaving the workshop. A variety of techniques was necessary in order to expand the Favrile range, and every conceivable metallic hue was therefore explored, from lustrous gold to pitted bronze, each identifiable by an evocative name such as Lava, Nacreous or Cypriot.

As a young man, Tiffany had been fascinated by the corroded appearance of certain examples of ancient Roman glass, which had taken on an iridescent sheen after having been buried in the earth for a long period. It was this challenge that gave rise to his first experiments in ornamental glass and some 20 pieces were shipped across the Atlantic in time for the opening exhibition of Siegfried Bing's new gallery in Paris. Bing had struck up a friendship with Tiffany on an earlier visit to New York and was astonished that '. . . after all the accomplishments of the Venetians, of Gallé and others, it was still possible to utilize glass in a new way that was often opaque and matt, with a surface like skin to the touch, silky and delicate'.

Tiffany's childhood had instilled in him a pragmatic approach to the world of commerce. He adopted a

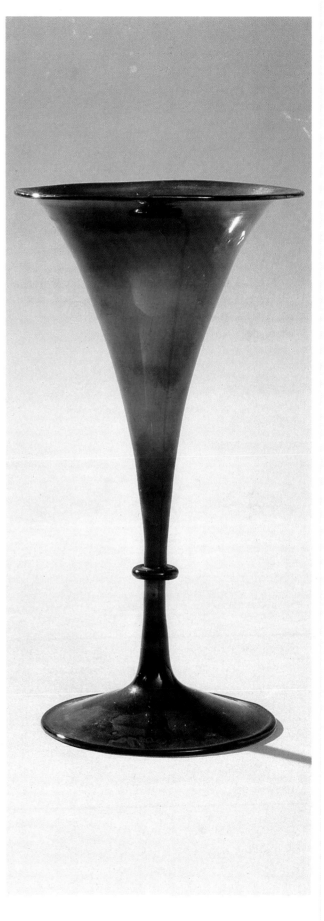

(LEFT) *Tiffany completed several major stained glass commissions including this window which was one of fifteen designed for the Old Blandford Church in Petersburgh, Virginia. They were erected as a memorial to the Confederate dead of the American Civil War.*

(RIGHT) *Karl Köpping epitomised the German* Jugendstil *spirit in a series of incredibly delicate glass vases. The vase illustrated was made by Friedrich Zitzmann, c.1900.*

typically American attitude to the creation of his art, which allowed no time for fanciful intellectual distractions. He enjoyed the heady world of business, and wholeheartedly embraced any possible commercial benefits modern technology could afford. He also surrounded himself with people of outstanding talent and allowed them the freedom to explore uncharted territory and exploit new opportunities, such as those offered by the innovative incandescent electric lamp, invented by Edison in 1885. Tiffany was probably the first to realize the exciting possibilities offered by this new medium and produced a range of table and standard lamps with exotic stained-glass shades. At their simplest, these designs can be read as an abstract depiction of nature based upon his favourite motifs of flowers and insects. Models included ivy, daffodils, geraniums, roses, pansies, lilies and butterflies. The two most famous, however, were the Dragonfly lamp, designed by Clara Driscoll and shown at Bing's shop in 1899 and again at the Paris Exposition Universelle of 1900, and the Wisteria Lamp, designed by Mrs Curtis Freschel in 1904.

(BELOW) *The Favrile range by Tiffany, exploited the brilliant hues possible with iridescent glass. The process entails the use of opalescent glass which has been treated with metallic oxides and heated in a controlled atmosphere to develop an iridescent sheen.*

(ABOVE) *Punch bowl by Tiffany in iridescent gold using non-lead glass; (height 15½in/315mm).*

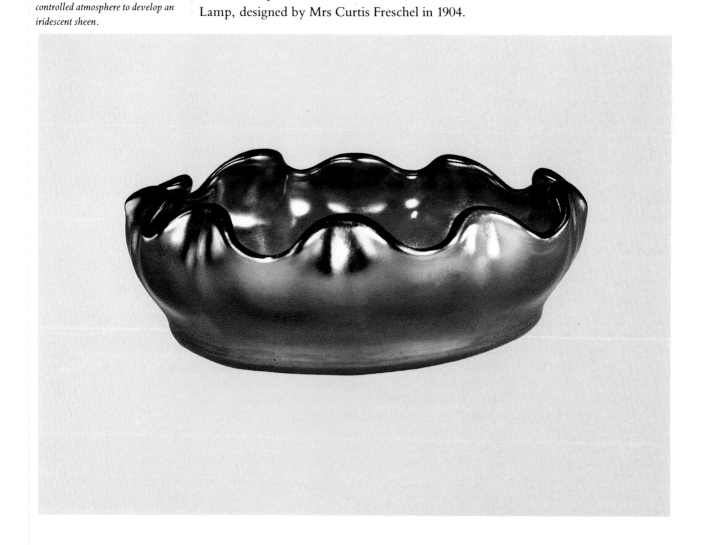

(RIGHT) *One of a series of very popular 'Jack-in-the-Pulpit' vases by Tiffany with the characteristic iridescent lustre; (height 19½in/ 485mm).*

A la Mode

The enormous commercial success of Tiffany spawned the usual legion of copyists and imitators. Although they were mostly American – such as Quezal Art Glass in Brooklyn, New York – European companies, too, were guilty of such practices, one being the firm of Johannes Loetz Witwe of Klostermühle in Bohemia which marketed its iridescent glassware as 'gläser à la Tiffany' and was assisted in this *hommage* by an ex-employee from the Corona factory. Europe did, however, produce other noteworthy glass artists exhibiting flair and originality. In Berlin, for example, Karl Köpping (1848–1914) developed a very pure form of

(BELOW) *The technique of iridescence was first developed commercially in 1863 by J. & L. Lobmeyr and was quickly taken up by several other European and American glasshouses. The selection illustrated has been attributed to the Loetz factory at Klostermühle, Austria.*

Art Nouveau glassmaking. His output usually comprized very slender and delicate thinly blown flower-like vessels and is often regarded as the epitome of the *Jugendstil*, or 'young style', the German equivalent of Gallic Art Nouveau.

In the traditional glass manufacturing city of Nancy, the example of Gallé had inspired the brothers Auguste (1853–1909) and Antonin (1864–1930) Daum to rechannel the bulk of the work produced in their father's glasshouse towards a more recognizable Art Nouveau style. They summed up their new approach in 1903 by enthusing about their '. . . study of living things, love of truth, a return of intellectualism, to poetic feeling in decoration, to logical principles of design and decoration'. They then set about refining the ancient technique of

(LEFT) *The success of the American glass industry was not restricted to Tiffany alone, but encompassed several other companies including Steuben and Quezal. The illustration shows examples of goblets and tumblers by all three companies, manufactured between 1900 and 1918.*

(RIGHT) *A marriage of opposites – wrought iron and glass: a collaborative venture between the Nancy glasshouse of Daum and the metal workshops of Majorelle; c.1920.*

(LEFT) *The sculptural quality of 'pâte-de-verre' glass was skilfully exploited by several Art Nouveau artists including Gabriel Argy-Rousseau and Almeric Walter.*

(BELOW) *A selection of glassware (1903–33) by the prominent American company of Steuben, founded in 1903 by Frederick Carder at Corning, New York.*

pâte-de-verre, which had been known originally to the early Egyptian artists but had been lost until 1885, when Henri Cros (1840–1907) rediscovered its formula while using the furnaces of the Sèvres porcelain factory.

The term *pâte-de-verre* literally means 'glass paste'; the result of the process is similar in appearance to alabaster. Its production was time-consuming: pre-manufactured powdered glass was combined with a binding agent and slowly heated before being fired in a mould. It was a technique fraught with difficulties because of the risk of cracking and also the danger of damage occurring both during the firing and also the annealing, or cooling, process. The first pieces produced by the Daum brothers date from 1906, when Alméric Walter (1859–1942), originally a ceramist, joined the firm. He spent several years with Daum, building up his knowledge of *pâte-de-verre* before breaking out on his own in 1919. He preferred to use a thicker, more robust form to ensure a higher rate of survival and achieved considerable fame in his own right.

As an expression of the Art Nouveau sensibility, glass was unrivalled among the applied arts. That quintessential quality of grace and freedom is best conveyed by this light, malleable material and this was especially evident in the hands of such master craftsmen as Gallé and Tiffany, who could effortlessly conjure up such evocative imagery. Any optimistic hope of a sustained progression of bold new ideas was, of course, cut short by the outbreak of World War I. However, the important first steps had already been taken: artists no longer considered glass a substitute for porcelain or rock crystal, to be incised or carved; instead they now looked to the intrinsic nature of the material as the key to its decoration.

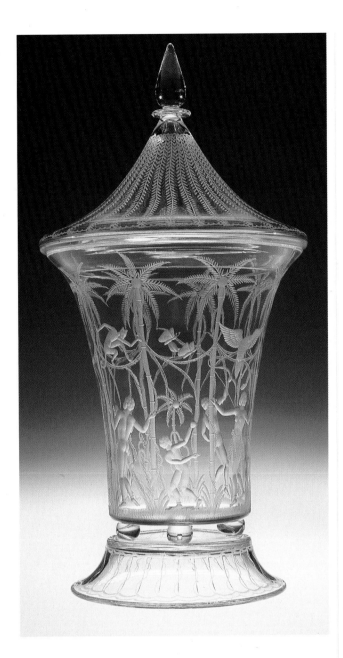

(ABOVE) The Negro Hut *(1918) by Eduard Hald for the Swedish company of Orrefors Glasbruk demonstrates the consummate skill of the engraver; (height 10½in/ 260mm, diameter 5½in/126mm).*

4

Art Deco and the Geometric

Camargue, *a boldly stylized Lalique vase (c.1935) with ribonny rim and base and a frosted-glass body decorated with four plaques. The horses are set against whirling clouds of dust or smoke stained in sepia.*

The period between the wars was one of the most exciting and inventive within the field of the decorative arts generally, and glass in particular. Often known as the Jazz Era or the Swing Era, it was a period obsessed with style and elegance – a time of conspicuous luxury and debilitating poverty; a time rocked by the Wall Street Crash of October 1929 and twisted by succeeding years of economic depression.

Many believe that such times of struggle and hardship generate a greater response from, and challenge to, the artist and designer. Others go further and suggest that the origins of 'design' itself date from the Great Depression of the 1920s and 1930s, when the increased competition for a steadily shrinking market gave rise to the idea of a corporate design policy to bolster the self-image of large organizations such as Ford, Texaco and Bell Telephone in the United States. Corporate consultants such as Norman Bel Geddes, Raymond Loewy and Henry Dreyfuss – all talented industrial designers – established the concepts of design and styling which were to herald the new technological age.

The unprecedented changes within society produced an equally vigorous response from the art world, and a succession of dynamic movements sprang up to challenge the status quo: the Cubists in France; the De Stijl group in Holland; the Constructivists in Russia; the Vorticists in England – all of which mounted concerted attacks on the complacency of middle-class values. Italy also reverberated with revolutionary fervour, and the

Futurists, led by the poet and publicist Filippo Marinetti, published their Manifesto in 1923, entitled *The Wireless Imagination*. It proclaimed that:

> Futurism is founded on the total revolution in human sensitivity that has taken place as a result of the great scientific discoveries. Those who make use today of the telegraph, telephone, gramophone, train, bicycle, motorcycle, automobile, transatlantic liner, airship, aeroplanes, cinematograph and daily newspaper do not realize that these different forms of communication, transportation and information exert a decisive influence on their psyche.

This concern was echoed in the concerted reaction against the florid exuberance of the Art Nouveau movement. There was an increasing tendency towards the abstraction of form and space in which line, colour and volume became the crucial elements in the manipulation of this space. The characteristics of new materials such as chrome and plastic allowed designers the opportunity to mimic the popular fascination for the express train and the ocean-going liner. Streamlining was therefore used extensively as a metaphor for speed and offered an innovative, fluid style for the new age.

(LEFT) *Vase (1915) by the Viennese architect Josef Hoffmann who preferred the geometric rather than the plant-like forms of his contemporaries; (height 5in/122mm).*

(ABOVE) *Light-green glass vase manufactured c.1915 by the Venetian firm of Salviati & Company. Its unusual form is reminiscent of some of today's more avant-garde pieces; (height 14½in/358mm, diameter 10½in/261mm).*

(RIGHT) *Small bowl (c.1920) by Gabriel Argy-Rousseau in pâte de verre with moth motif; (height 3½in/76mm).*

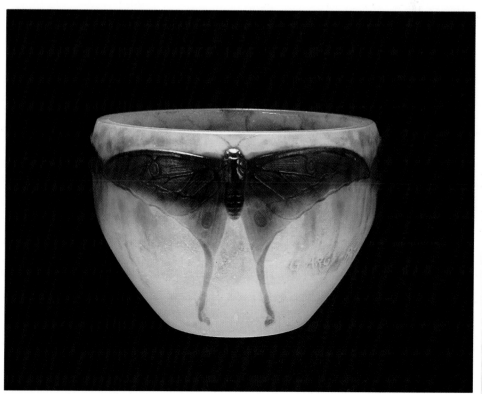

French pre-eminence

Much of the decorative art dating from between the two world wars is now classified as Art Deco, a term which was coined only in the 1960s and is taken from the title of the exhibition held in Paris in 1925, L'Exposition Internationale des Arts Décoratifs et Industriels Modernes. This grand affair to celebrate the unrivalled position of French craftsmanship within the decorative arts grew out of the phenomenal success of the 1900 Exposition Universelle, which had attracted a staggering 50 million visitors over the six months of its duration. The Société des Artistes-Décorateurs had been specifically set up to organize the second of such events, but was prevented from doing so by the outbreak of World War I.

The 1925 Exposition proved as successful as that of 1900, its influence such that it provided the impetus for the dispersal of the Art Deco aesthetic throughout the developed world. Paris was the acknowledged epicentre of this brash new movement. This bustling metropolis offered a haven not only for revolutionary painters such as Pablo Picasso, Georges Braque and Fernand Léger, but also an established network of workshops and willing craftsmen, skilled in the manufacture of the

applied arts. French expertise embraced all the decorative arts, including cabinetmaking, jewellery and glass-blowing. The 1925 Exposition was intended to consolidate their high reputation beyond any doubt and was therefore treated by the French authorities as no mere trade fair but an encapsulation of an emerging industrial civilization.

This view was reinforced by the wide and varied range of glass on display. Manufacturers included the Daum brothers, significant makers of Art Nouveau glass, but who had subsequently altered their stylistic approach to parallel the new tastes in design. The two principal figures, however, were Maurice Marinot (1882–1960) and René Lalique (1860–1945). These two men personified the ideological divergence that became increasingly apparent in the course of this period. The role of glass was torn between its use as an artistic medium for individual expression and its place as an expensive industrially produced multiple. Marinot championed the notion of the dedicated craftsman toiling over the hot furnace to capture his creative vision, whereas Lalique embodied the seemingly contradictory concept of the artistically talented entrepreneur producing glassware in volume for the domestic market. Both men were French by birth and their separate biographies reflect this deep schism within the glass industry.

MARINOT:

....

'this new game'

Marinot was born in the town of Troyes, and in 1898 he entered the famous Ecole des Beaux-Arts to pursue his love of painting and sculpture. The established structure of this institution restricted his more intuitive spirit and he looked instead to his contemporaries for a more purposeful direction. This he found as a minor member of the group known as *Les Fauves*, who achieved considerable notoriety after their first public showing as part of the Salon d'Automne exhibition in 1905. This loosely connected collection of artists included Henri Matisse and André Derain, and had been christened *Les Fauves*, literally 'the wild beasts', because of their brutal use of simplified shapes and brash colours.

Marinot's development as a painter, however, was irrevocably curtailed on an informal visit to the small

'THE FRAGILE BEAUTY OF THE FEMME FATALE'

Many look upon the Art Deco era as a period of sublime decadence, while the cult of nostalgia evokes an image of Hollywood starlets and jazz music, streamlined elegance and smokey cabaret bars. This romanticized notion is given additional credence by much of the glass of the period and many artists – such as Lalique, Descomps and Argy-Rousseau – explored the perennial fascination for the female form. Their model of feminine beauty was the 'dancer', who was invariably either partly or completely naked and could suggest the exotic, the mysterious, the *femme fatale*.

(FAR LEFT) *Cast glass sculpture (c.1927) by Gabriel Argy-Rousseau.*

(LEFT) *Glass sculpture (c.1925) by Jean Descomps and Almeric Walter.*

(FAR LEFT) *Designed by the Swedish artist E. Stromberg in 1930, the spherical form is accentuated by the use of grey-tinted glass for the chequered pattern.*

(RIGHT) *One of a pair of glass bookends in the form of two turkeys by Maurice-Ernest Sabino; c.1925.*

(ABOVE) *Decanter with stopper (1922) by Maurice Marinot, displaying a more refined use of hand-painted enamel decoration; (height 8½in/210mm, diameter 2½in/55mm).*

glassworks of the Viard brothers at Bar-sur-Seine, near his family's estate. It was his first glimpse of the sheer physical effort necessary to blow glass, combined with the extremes of temperature and colour, which stunned him into '. . . a violent desire for this new game'. He immediately commissioned the brothers to manufacture some bottles and vases to his own design, intending to decorate them himself. These early experiments merely transferred his painterly skills from canvas to a new medium: glass. The initial shapes were invariably simple, with bold, stylized flowers and figures sketched onto the flat or curved surfaces in brightly coloured, vitreous enamel paints. He anxiously exhibited the first few pieces in 1912, but these drew limited praise. One exception was the critic Léon Rosenthal, who reviewed Marinot's work for the *Gazette des Beaux-Arts*, saying that 'it has been a long time since an innovation of such importance has come to enrich the art of glass'.

In the following year, 1913, some of Marinot's paintings travelled to the United States, where they formed part of the highly influential Armory Show in New York. This exhibition introduced the most radical of the European avant-garde to an unsuspecting and deeply conservative American public. Recent paintings by Matisse, Duchamp and the German Expressionists

(ABOVE) *Vessel (c.1924) by Maurice Marinot in clear glass which has been acid-etched and enamelled; (height 8½in/213mm, diameter 6½in/155mm).*

shocked both critics and public alike. For many the work seemed to trample on conventional notions of beauty and depict only what was ugly and deformed. One such outraged visitor was Louis Comfort Tiffany, who had been horrified and saddened at such 'progressive' tendencies which could allow the human figure to be reduced to what he saw as a crude, angular agglomeration of geometric shapes.

Marinot had by now all but given up painting and instead turned his full attention to learning the traditional skills of the glassmaker. He was unhappy using applied decoration and felt that it rendered the medium almost irrelevant, so he set about working on the glassblower's bench. He was over 30 years old at the time and reflected: 'Everything I have done, I have done with difficulty.' His apprenticeship had barely started before he was conscripted to fight in World War I. Marinot later returned to his workbench with renewed vigour and determination to explore the sculptural possibilities of this most malleable of mediums. His interest lay in manipulating the hot molten metal in the flames of the furnace and he was enraptured by the elemental quality of fire to create such monumental, yet dynamic shapes in liquid glass. His skill lay in mastering the technical problems of harnessing colour, texture and mass in order to capture that poetical abstraction between light and form which was possible only in glass.

Marinot's philosophy was clearly set out in an article he wrote for *The Studio* magazine in 1927, wherein he stated that:

To be a glass-maker is to blow transparent matter by the side of a blinding furnace . . . to shape sensitive material into simple lines by a rhythm suited to the very nature of glass, so as to rediscover later in the bright immobility of the ware the life which has breathed it into a fitting decorative form. This decorative form will be worthy of respect, or something more, as it bodies forth in proportion the two significant qualities of glass: transparency and lustre. I think that a good piece of glassware preserves, at its best, a form reflecting the human breath which has shaped it, and that its shape must be a moment in the life of the glass fixed in the instant of cooling.

He usually worked diligently on his own in a quiet corner of the Viard brothers' glassworks. It was here that he refined his artistic ability and produced a series of massive thick-walled jars, vases and stoppered bottles. These fall into two distinct categories: firstly, the smooth-sided objects of layered glass which employed a variety of internal chemical effects, such as air bubbles, streaks of muted colour or smoky tints, and, secondly,

(RIGHT) *As Marinot's passion and skill for working glass at the edge of the furnace developed, his work became much more modelled and sculptural. The vessel illustrated was made c.1934; (height 7in/ 170mm).*

the deeply etched, chunky vessels modelled with aggressive geometric patterns formed by their repeated immersion in hydrofluoric acid. The outer surfaces of the latter pieces were often polished to heighten the contrast in texture.

His work was immensely popular and featured regularly in the popular art journals and newspapers of the day. His fame reached its zenith in 1925, when his one-off creations appeared prominently not only at the Paris Exposition, but also at New York's Museum of Modern Art, where he was afforded the rare honour of a retrospective exhibition during his own lifetime. Twelve years later, at the 1937 Paris Internationale Exposition, he was awarded the supreme overall prize. Sadly, this proved to be his last exhibition of glass because the Viard workshops closed later that year; and a far greater tragedy was to come.

Marinot was no longer a young man and had retired to his paints when his atelier was bombed during an Allied air attack in 1944; several thousand drawings and some 2,500 paintings were destroyed, along with most of his glass. Fortunately, some pieces did survive and are now safely housed in several of the larger museums and cultural institutions around the world. The little of his work remaining in private hands appears only very rarely at auction and can command enormous prices.

This accidental scarcity of available glass is not the case with the work of that other seminal figure from the Art Deco era, René Lalique. He achieved possibly one of the most difficult of all creative tasks, namely, the successful marriage of art and commerce. Lalique's was unquestionably the most accomplished of all the industrially orientated glasshouses and still boasts an impressive showroom on the prestigious Rue Royale in Paris.

LALIQUE:

. . . .

'Luxury goods and Consummate craftsmanship

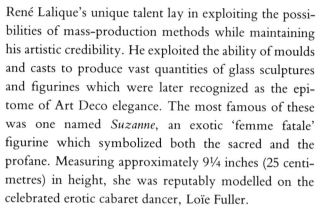

René Lalique's unique talent lay in exploiting the possibilities of mass-production methods while maintaining his artistic credibility. He exploited the ability of moulds and casts to produce vast quantities of glass sculptures and figurines which were later recognized as the epitome of Art Deco elegance. The most famous of these was one named *Suzanne*, an exotic 'femme fatale' figurine which symbolized both the sacred and the profane. Measuring approximately 9¼ inches (25 centimetres) in height, she was reputably modelled on the celebrated erotic cabaret dancer, Loïe Fuller.

Lalique himself was born in 1860, in the small town of Ay-sur-Marne in France. As a boy he was a naturally gifted draughtsman and at the age of 16 was offered an apprenticeship with the celebrated goldsmith Louis Aucoc, who, although unoriginal in style, enjoyed no small reputation making neo-Rococo jewellery for a select circle of very wealthy clients in Paris. Lalique later

(LEFT) *Marinot produced a series of flasks which, although incredibly simple in form, possessed great clarity and an element of the monumental.*

(ABOVE AND RIGHT) *The relationship between sculpture and glass has always been somewhat ambiguous, however, many artists have successfully exploited the inherent characteristics of the latter to inform the former. The illustration is by the French artist Colotte and titled* Head of a Man *(1931).*

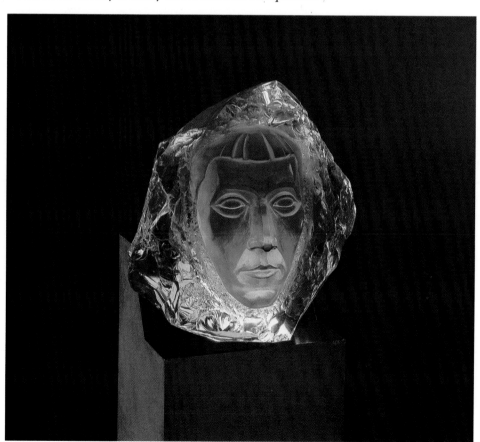

CIRE-PERDUE, THE LOST-WAX METHOD

It was during his first success as a jeweller that Lalique used glass, often ordinary cut-glass, in juxtaposition with more expensive semiprecious stones. As a result of this initial interest in the medium, he decided to open a small glass workshop at Clairfontaine, some 25 miles southwest of Paris, where he employed four assistants to supervise the manufacture of sculptural vases using the *cire-perdue*, or lost-wax, method. In this process a wax model was carved and then encased in a plaster mould; the wax was then melted, drained, and replaced by molten glass which was then allowed to set before the mould was finally broken open to release the finished object. A high degree of fine detail could be achieved using this technique and the breaking of each mould ensured that each piece was unique. Some of Lalique's early experiments in *cire-perdue* glass were first exhibited at the Turin Exposition of 1902 and caused considerable excitement at the time.

(TOP LEFT) *Vase by Rene Lalique illustrating the depth of relief possible with the cire-perdue method.*

(LEFT) *Two vases from 1926 by Lalique with heavily sculptured bases; one with rose blossom, the second with fish amid frothing waves.*

(TOP RIGHT) *Etched figure painted in black 'speaking no evil' (1930) by the Swedish designer Vicke Lindstrand.*

studied silversmithing in England for two years before returning again to Paris. His skills were very much in demand and his reputation such that he soon began working as a freelance designer not only in jewellery but also in fabrics and wallpapers.

Lalique was by now very much a cult figure in the heady world of fin-de-siècle Paris. He enjoyed the patronage of Siegfried Bing and exhibited frequently in his Maison de l'Art Nouveau. He also produced a great volume of work for the rich and famous, including the actress Sarah Bernhardt, the petroleum magnate Calouste Gulbenkian and the Rothschild family. Lalique's work as a jewellery designer was strongly Art Nouveau in both style and spirit, and he created some very dramatic, organic pieces which received considerable acclaim at the 1900 Paris Exposition. Indeed, his reputation was

such that he even received the coveted Légion d'Honneur for his skills as a goldsmith.

He set up his first shop in 1905 at 24 Place Vendôme, very near the premises of the famous perfumer, François Coty. The following year Coty approached his neighbour and commissioned Lalique to redesign his graphics. This initial brief was quickly expanded to include the design of a 'tasteful yet simple container' for the launch of his new perfume. This modest request opened up a vast new market for Lalique and led to numerous other commissions from Roger et Gallet, Worth, Forvil, D'Orsay and many other perfumers. This enduring affair with scent bottles has entailed the manufacture of literally millions of glass vessels and continues even today with the company Cristal Lalique, headed by the master's granddaughter, Marie-Claude Lalique.

The scale of such a large operation necessitated the purchase of the Verrerie de Combe-la-Ville, near Fontainebleau, in 1909. This was forced to close down during World War I, but following the Armistice Lalique shifted to an even larger glassworks at Wingen-sur-Moder in the Alsace region. This already well-established factory provided him with the experienced work force capable of achieving the highest quality control, a vital element if he was to maintain his position as the premier manufacturer of mass-produced glass objects. This new base allowed him to expand his portfolio to include mirrors, picture frames, paperweights, goblets, plates, inkwells, ashtrays, statuettes, clock cases, lamps, chandeliers and even furniture. This vast range of products was possible only because of his continual refinement of the manufacturing process. He employed various techniques such as pressing and mould blowing, but also developed the concept of centrifugal casting, whereby the mould is spun at high speed forcing the molten glass into every concavity, no matter how deep.

In addition to the above, Lalique also secured several highly prestigious commissions for the grand trans-oceanic liners such as the *Paris* in 1920, the *Ile de France* in 1927 and the *Normandie* in 1935. His position was therefore highly esteemed by the time of the 1925 Paris Exposition, which served to confirm his reputation as the most inventive and successful glassmaker of his day. He was also honoured with a major retrospective exhi-

(BELOW) *Art Deco hand-painted glass bowl by Quezal Art Glass and Decorating Co. of Brooklyn, New York; (c.1925).*

(RIGHT) *Grande Boulle Lierre (1921) by Rene Lalique in frosted glass with sparse, yet dramatic, ivy leaf design. This was one of his largest vases, measuring some 14in/350mm in height.*

bition at the Musée des Arts Décoratifs in Paris in 1933, but he was by then over 70 years old and plagued by a debilitating form of arthritis. Nonetheless, his business swelled to over 600 employees and he managed to work until 1939, when war again forced him to close down the glassworks.

René Lalique died in 1945, bequeathing a considerable legacy to the world of glass. His unique contribution was to elevate design beyond the organic, beyond the *hommage à nature* ideology of Art Nouveau. Instead, he

instilled a more rigorous, more organized approach which helped carry design into the new century and at the same time encapsulated the Art Deco maxim of 'luxury goods fashioned with consummate craftsmanship'. The Art Deco aesthetic could be seen as an inspired amalgam of Classical and Egyptian motifs fused with the tribal arts of Africa and the Cubists' perception of geometric form. The enormous success of such radical artists as Marinot and Lalique was all the more remarkable, given the general economic slump within the glass

(RIGHT) *Although among the smaller items in Lalique's vast oeuvre, his perfume bottles represent the perfect marriage of high design standards and inexpensive mass production. The design of the 'Panier de Roses' flacon dates from c.1910; (height 4in/100mm).*

(FAR RIGHT) *Vase in amber glass (c.1920) with gilded frieze by Ludwig Moser & Söhn; (height 3¹⁄₂in/81mm).*

glass. His work, which had been so popular with the previous generation, now fell into disfavour and was dismissed as old-fashioned. Steuben, who had copied the Tiffany style for many years and had produced an immense variety of highly coloured, lustreware objects, also suffered some fallow years due to this shift in popular tastes. In the mid-1930s, however, Steuben abandoned this approach and instead adopted an adventurous new policy of inviting leading figures from the international art world to lend their considerable credibility to the firm and help promote sales to a wider international market. The company developed a high-grade crystal and concentrated on simple but bold blown forms which were then engraved to the artists' design. Some 27 different artists were involved in this initial collaboration, including Henri Matisse, Jean Cocteau, Eric Gill and Georgia O'Keeffe.

This inspired coupling of art and commerce proved overwhelmingly successful and was repeated some 14 years later in 1954, when a group of 20 influential British artists, among them Graham Sutherland, John Piper and Lawrence Whistler, were invited to transfer their artistic vision onto glass. Such enlightened ideas earned Steuben considerable prestige and a reputation for skilfully combining design with craftsmanship. Darker developments in Europe, however, were soon to shatter such simple notions of harmony and beauty.

industry itself. Their great popularity inspired numerous imitators, of course, in both Europe and North America. In France, there were André Hunebelle, Etling and Maurice-Ernest Sabino; in Great Britain, the company of James A Jobling; and in the United States, the firm of Steuben Glass.

Founded in upstate Corning, New York, 1903 by British-born Frederick Carder (1864–1963) with the express purpose of producing ornamental glassware, Steuben was bought over in 1918 by the massive Corning Glass Works from New York to be reorganized as their Art Glass department. The death of Louis Comfort Tiffany in 1933 marked the end of an era for American

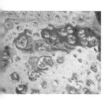

5

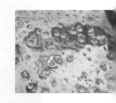

Modernism

Claret jug with pear shaped glass body on three legs by Christopher Dresser, c.1879. Dresser is one designer who truly merits the description 'a man ahead of his time'.

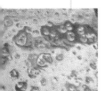

The influence of the Art Deco Movement generated a definite homogeneity of design between the larger developed countries of the world. This tendency in turn gave birth to the Modern Movement during the 1920s and 1930s and the crystallization of an international style after World War II. The utilitarian roots of Modernism can be seen in a great variety of vernacular objects made during the 19th century. Many common household items, including furniture, ceramic and glass, embodied (if only subconsciously) the teachings of 18th-century British philosophers such as David Hume, who argued eloquently for the intrinsic worth of utility and function.

This call was echoed in the United States by Horatio Greenough who demanded in his book, *Travels, Observations and Experiences of a Yankee Stonecutter*, published in 1852, that '. . . the redundant must be pared down, the superfluous dropped, the necessary itself reduced to its simplest expression and then we shall find, whatever the organization may be, that beauty was waiting for us'.

DRESSER:

the harbinger of functionalism

The dictates of Functionalism required that the design of any object must reflect only its utilitarian purpose, and divest itself of any extraneous decoration. One of the early pioneers of this austere approach was the Scottish designer Christopher Dresser (1834–1904), who worked primarily in metal and glass. Dresser was born in Glasgow, then the prosperous second city of the British Empire. The father of 13 children, he was also the author of several learned treatises on the principles of art and design. The most influential of these was his *Principles of Decorative Design*, first published in 1873, in which he set down his requirements for the design and manufacture of glass: 'If a material is worked in its most simple and befitting manner, the results obtained are more beautiful than those which are arrived at by any roundabout method of production . . . If the objects formed result from the easiest methods of working the material, and are such as perfectly answer the end proposed by their information, and are beautiful, nothing more can be expected of them.'

This modus operandi obviously embraced the use of machinery, thus eschewing the medieval stance of William Morris, who was an exact contemporary of Dresser. There were, however, several common threads which linked their individual philosophies of design: both men saw Nature as the key to ornamentation; both drew inspiration from botany and the study of plant forms; both also looked to history for ideas, but for Morris this was to fulfil an impossible yearning to retreat to medieval times, while for Dresser it was to spark ideas for the present. He argued that '. . . ornament is that which, superadded to utility, renders the object more acceptable through bestowing upon it an amount of beauty that it would not otherwise possess . . . There can be morality or immorality in art, the utterance of truth or of falsehood; and by his art the ornamentist may exalt or debase a nation.'

Although many of Dresser's basic tenets contradicted those of Morris, they were equally unpopular with the general public, who held with the status quo of heavy ornate Victoriana. His shop, which opened in 1880 in New Bond Street, London, enjoyed a somewhat precarious financial existence. It was called the Art Furnishers' Alliance and provided a valuable retail outlet for

Dresser's own designs in furniture, metalwork, ceramics, textiles and glass. The bold forms and simplicity of line which characterize much of Dresser's work predate by some 50 years much of what was to be produced by the Bauhaus School in Germany. Dresser championed the Ruskinian tenet that a material's inherent qualities must be respected and expressed honestly. The fluid ductility found in the metal of molten glass was therefore the principal tool of the designer; all surplus ornamentation was to be abandoned. Dresser's work in glass during the decade 1885 to 1895 offers a textbook demonstration of this principle. This period included designs for the 'Clutha' range of glass manufactured by James Couper & Sons of Glasgow (the term 'Clutha' was derived from an archaic name for the River Clyde). The flowing curves and sweeping lines of the Clutha range were almost Art Nouveau in spirit, while the composition of the glass itself was enlivened by including subtle streaks of contrasting colours, lines of trapped air bubbles and tiny flecks of metal foil, all of which added richness and

(LEFT) *Tall goose-necked vase (c.1895) in pale green Clutha glass with pink striations by Dresser; (height 12in/375mm).*

(BELOW) *The work of Christopher Dresser prefigures the introduction of Modernism by some 30 years by stripping design of all superfluous ornamentation. Instead he relied upon the inherent qualities of the material to give it 'honest' beauty, as can be seen in the cruet set and soup tureen he designed for the Birmingham firm of Hukin & Heath Ltd (c.1877).*

variety to the finished object.

Dresser's earlier work, with the Birmingham firm of Hukin & Heath, often involved a combination of metal with glass and included a series of cruet sets, decanters, claret jugs, drinking glasses and the like. Perhaps his most prophetic work was a range of electroplated silverware he designed in the late 1870s for James Dixon & Sons of Sheffield. These consisted of a number of tea and coffee pots which were designed as severe, prismatic forms, completely unadorned and stripped of any extraneous decoration – the epitome of the Functionalist aesthetic. This hybrid assemblage of geometric elements prefigures the Modernists' obsession with Platonic forms: the cone, the cylinder, the pyramid, the sphere and the cube. This purity of form and economy of line reflected Dresser's belief that form should follow function. It was essential that '. . . all decorated objects should appear to be what they are; they should not pretend to be what they are not'. Although Dresser died only four years into the new century, he proved a watershed between the 19th-century craving for ornamentation and the most rigorous dictates of the Machine Age. Such a radical vision can also be seen in the work of his Glaswegian compatriot, Charles Rennie Mackintosh (1868–1928), whose influence was particularly strong in the Austrian capital, Vienna.

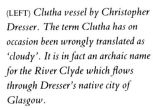

(LEFT) *Clutha vessel by Christopher Dresser. The term Clutha has on occasion been wrongly translated as 'cloudy'. It is in fact an archaic name for the River Clyde which flows through Dresser's native city of Glasgow.*

HOFFMAN

. . . .

The Vienna workshops

(ABOVE) *Clutha glass bowl (c.1904) made by the Glasgow firm of James Couper & Sons, set within a pewter stand probably designed by Archibald Knox for the London department store of Liberty.*

Fin-de-siècle Vienna was no stranger to revolutionary ideas and ranks alongside Berlin and Paris as the birthplace of Modernism. The liberal attitudes of the day engendered considerable intellectual debate within the city and it was home at various times to several of the greatest thinkers and artists of the century: among them Sigmund Freud, the composers Gustav Mahler and Arnold Schoenberg, the painters Gustav Klimt and Egon Schiele, and the architects Adolf Loos and Otto Wagner.

The formation of the Secessionist movement in 1898 provided a focus for a group of radical young artists who were disenchanted with established values and wanted to forge a new awareness within art. Their regular exhibitions offered a vehicle for this disquiet and encouraged a heightened concern for art and aesthetics. Their Eighth Exhibition, in 1900, included works by various avant-garde artists from abroad, including CR Ashbee, Charles Rennie Mackintosh and his wife Margaret Macdonald Mackintosh, as well as noted

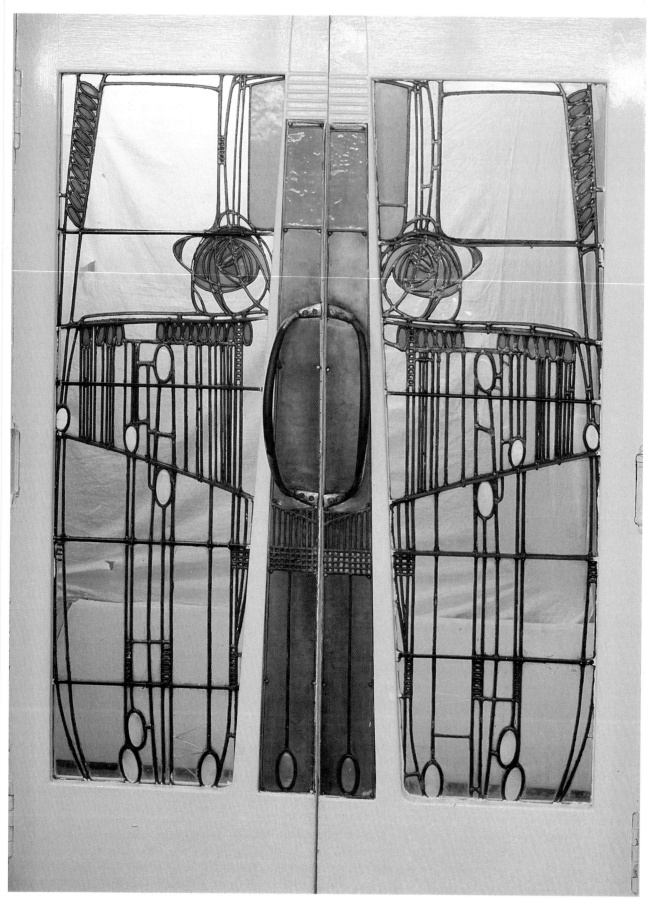

Viennese artists/craftsmen such as Josef Hoffmann and Koloman Moser. It was Hoffmann and Moser who, with the financial backing of Fritz Waerndorfer, were to found the Wiener Werkstätte, the Vienna Workshops, in 1903.

The cultural dialogue and spiritual bond between the two cities of Vienna and Glasgow were reinforced by Hoffmann's visit to Scotland to seek out the advice of Mackintosh on the setting up of the Wiener Werkstätte. He demanded bluntly that '. . . every object that leaves your hand must carry the outspoken mark of individuality, beauty and the most exact execution . . . Begin today! If I was in Vienna I would help with a very strong shovel.'

Hoffmann's enthusiasm for a viable hand-crafted alternative to shoddy mass-produced items was encapsulated in a questioning article which he wrote for the magazine *Das Interieur*, published in 1901, in which he asked: 'How can we create a new tradition if we cannot find followers in this poorest period of all time? We should start again at the very point where personal creativity had come to an end. Have we missed this possibility already? Didn't we have the same predecessors as they had in England?'

Hoffmann was the driving intellectual force behind the formation of the Wiener Werkstätte, his principal goal being to develp an uncluttered approach to design which would prioritize decoration as an integral element, not simply a cosmetic afterthought. The Wiener Werkstätte consisted of a small nucleus of creative artists and time-served craftsmen working side by side to produce

(LEFT) *The celebrated Scottish designer Charles Rennie Mackintosh was concerned not only with the architecture of the exterior, but also with the architecture of the interior, as can be seen in his design for the Willow Tearooms (1901–04) at 199 Sauchiehall Street, Glasgow.*

(BELOW) *The Austrian architect/ designer Josef Hoffmann was greatly influenced by Mackintosh and shared his belief in simplicity of both line and form. The glass illustrated was designed for the Wiener Werkstätte in 1915.*

hand-finished items which would aspire towards a more harmonious, more geometric modern style.

Hoffmann believed that '. . . our strength has to lie in good proportions and materials well-handled', and consequently the early years reflected this personal ideology, resulting in a somewhat austere, rectilinear, neofunctional style which was meticulously crafted and beautifully balanced. The noble ideals of the Werkstätte were eloquently summed up in their Working Programme of 1905, which is worth quoting at length:

> The immeasurable harm caused in the realm of arts and crafts by shoddy mass-production on the one hand, and mindless imitation of old styles on the other, has swept through the entire world like a huge flood. We have lost touch with the culture of our forebears and are tossed about by a thousand contradictory whims and demands. In most cases the machine has replaced the hand and the businessman had taken the craftsman's place. It would be madness to swim against this current. All this notwithstanding, we have founded our workshop. It exists to provide on native soil a point of repose amid the cheerful noise of craftsmanship at work and to give comfort to all who accept the message of Ruskin and Morris . . . The worth of artistic work and of inspiration must be recognized and prized once again. The work of the art craftsman is to be measured by the same yardstick as that of the painter and the sculptor.

The ambitious nature of such a manifesto encouraged the Wiener Werkstätte to explore every area of the applied arts, and their portfolio came to include architectural interiors, furnishings, decorative paintings, sculpture, graphics, ceramics, jewellery, textiles, wallpaper, haute couture, mosaics, bookbinding, cutlery, tableware and postcards. In the field of architecture their most prestigious commission was from the Belgian financier, Adolphe Stoclet, who in 1905 invited the Werkstätte to design, decorate, furnish and equip his lavish new residence in the suburbs of Brussels, the Palais Stoclet. This early success was then quickly followed by an invitation to exhibit at the influential 1914 Werkbund Exhibition held at Cologne.

Much of the Werkstätte's output involved a joint collaboration between the designer of the object and the person who carried out the decoration. This was particularly so in the production of glassware, which first had to be manufactured by established factories, mainly Bohemian, such as J. & L. Lobmeyr, Loetz and Meyr's Neffe, before being hand-finished in their own workshops by one of the artisans, for example, Dagobert Peche. The particular appeal of glass for the Werkstätte

(LEFT) *Blue glass vase (1920) by Josef Hoffmann, who had moved progressively away from the more severe, geometric forms to develop a restrained version of the neo-classical.*

(BELOW LEFT) *Set of glasses designed by Josef Hoffmann for Lobmeyr (c.1910). Of all the Austrian firms for whom the members of the Werkstätte designed, Lobmeyr was considered the most prestigious.*

was reflected in this florid extract from their jubilee catalogue of 1928, written by Leopold Rochowanski:

> Glass objects represent a personalized perception of space. As though born of brightness, if placed in a bright light, they will set a rhythm for the dancing light, or catch a moment's repose for converging light beams. Snatched from the unending stream of time, they unfold the limpid purity of a festive day.

The Werkstätte's principal designers in glass were Otto Prutscher (1880–1949), Koloman Moser (1868–1918) and Josef Hoffmann (1870–1956), whose varied talents encompassed both the playful neo-Baroque and the more severe, geometric Moderne. The range of objects included tumblers, glasses, vases, cups, bowls and boxes, but their strange unfamiliar shapes, and their designers' somewhat estranged views on aesthetics, limited their appeal to only a tiny enlightened minority of the wealthy Viennese bourgeoisie. They strove for '. . . good and beautiful work rather than financial success' and this wilful disregard for the harsh realities of commerce only hastened their inevitable economic collapse. The company closed down in 1932.

The anti-industrial stance adopted by the Wiener Werkstätte was not universally shared. The Deutscher Werkbund, for example, was founded in Munich in 1907 with the express intention of '. . . enhancing the position of craftsmanship through co-operation between art, industry and handicraft'. The Werkbund proved highly influential in changing people's attitudes towards a greater philosophical acceptance of the logic of the machine-made object. This controversial role for industrial production was championed by Theodore Fischer, who declared that '. . . it is not the machine that is responsible for poor quality work but our incapacity to use it effectively'. The Werkbund brought together for the first time craftsmen, designers and industrialists to seek practical, ideologically sound solutions to the problems of 'good design'.

The main topic of debate was that of *Sachlichkeit* a term which has no proper English equivalent but means practicality or matter-of-factness, and focused attention on the conundrum of 'Form follows Function'. This dictate, coined by the American architect Louis Sullivan, was soon to become the battle cry of the emerging Modern Movement. The Werkbund, in turn, called for 'Form without Ornament' and organized an exhibition in 1924 to propagate their message. This exhibition toured both Europe and North America and was highly influential as a catalyst in the realization of Modernism, the roots of which can be traced to the Viennese architect Adolf Loos (1870–1933), who castigated ornament as a 'crime'. Loos believed that the rational process behind Functionalism would generate a style beyond style, possessing a purity of form and clarity of concept and construction which would lead to a world of permanently valid forms where nothing could be improved upon, nothing replaced, nothing renewed.

(RIGHT) *Heavy glass vessel by Gunnel Nyman enlivened only by a carefully orchestrated pattern of air bubbles and manufactured by the Notsjö Glassworks, Nuutajärvo, Finland, in the early 1940s.*

BAUHAUS

. . . .

objects for the 'emancipated proletariat'

It was amid such Utopian optimism that the famous Bauhaus School was inaugurated in 1919, with Walter Gropius (1883–1969) as its first director.

The Staatliches Bauhaus, or State Architectural Institute, was located first at Weimar and later at Dessau, now part of East Germany. It was an amalgamation of two separate schools, of fine art and the arts and crafts, fused together to form a single, forward-looking centre of excellence. The school's manifesto established its aim:

(BELOW) *Bauhaus design by Josef Albers; after the school had moved from Weimar to Dessau, Albers ran the Department of Interior Design with Alfred Arndt.*

(RIGHT) *A classic Modernist interior, geometric and devoid of ornament, c.1930. This was the Bauhaus vision of the future for the 'emancipated proletariat'.*

The finished goods were ultimately intended to '. . . adorn the house of the emancipated proletariat'. Such philanthropic social aspirations underpinned the basic course structure and informed the wide range of workshop activities, which included metalwork, pottery, weaving, typography, wall-painting, cabinetmaking and stained glass. It was here that the early concepts of Modernism were given concrete form; where the dilemma between standardization and individuality, machine and hand-crafts, was systematically analyzed; where, arguably, modern design was born.

The pioneering work of the Bauhaus contributed more than any other single institution to the establishment of a new order in cultural values. Such a radical vision, however, unsettled the ruling German National Socialist Party and the school was raided by police and storm-troopers on April 11 1933 and forced to close down under the spurious pretext that the school had printed and circulated Communist propaganda. Many of the more celebrated figures had by this time already fled, first to Great Britain and eventually to the United States, where they propagated the Bauhaus philosophy across the industrialized world.

to create a new guild of craftsmen . . . to create the new buildings of the future, which will embrace architecture and sculpture and paintings and which will rise one day towards heaven from the hands of a million workers like the crystal symbolism of a new faith.

This vision promulgated by the Bauhaus was the first real fusion of art and design with industry. The broad-based curriculum brought all the arts together under one banner, where '. . . architects, sculptors, painters should all get back to the craft. Art is no longer a profession. There is no qualitative difference between artist and craftsman. The artist is only a craftsman writ large.'

Such radical educational ideas attracted the core of Europe's avant garde as tutors; men such as Paul Klee, Wassily Kandinsky, Oskar Schlemmer, Marcel Breuer, László Moholy-Nagy, Johannes Itten and Ludwig Mies van der Rohe (1886–1969), who was to be appointed its third director in 1930. Students were encouraged to exploit the potential benefits of industrial production methods. Objects were therefore reduced to simple elemental components suitable for machine manufacture.

6

Postwar Optimism and the Individual

The colourful exuberance of Italian post-war design: none of the 'bareness . . . and impersonality' of Modernism that Stephen Spender so despised.

In tandem with the Bauhaus, the Deutscher Werkbund was also forced into temporary exile until after World War II, when it was reconvened and set about the task of defining the 'object'. A diverse group of individuals and officials was hurriedly organized into a Council of Industrial Form, which eventually issued a ruling which specified that '. . . the object as a whole must have no expressive feature which is not in accordance with the purposes for which the object is intended'.

Such a rigid definition soon provoked the inevitable backlash, and by the late 1930s, the Modern Movement was long past; the neo-Functionalist dogma of the 1920s and 1930s was now considered somewhat tired, even old-fashioned. The Bauhaus ideology, which had set out to develop a definitive style to overthrow all previous styles, had failed. In its place was something called the 'Bauhaus Style', which was both recognizable and distinctive, to such an extent that by the late 1950s it had already been allocated a slot in the chronological history of design movements. The outmoded values of the Functionalist tradition were now considered highly questionable, and this doubt was summarized by the writer Stephen Spender, who despised its '. . . bareness, simplicity, squareness or roundness, solidity, seriousness and impersonality'.

The collapse of Modernism as the driving force within design was due to many factors, the most compelling being that many now felt it to be cold and emotionally barren. This factor, coupled with the drift away from organized religion (so prevalent at the time), gave rise to the notion of redemption, not through the church, but through the hand-crafted object. This phenomenon was particularly evident in the United States, where the transcendental writings of Ralph Waldo Emerson and Walt Whitman were so popular. Their search for spiritual values inspired many idealistic postwar artists to strive for a higher plane of consciousness and led to a greater need for artistic self-expression.

Practicality was no longer the principal goal and the emphasis shifted instead to the abstract, or sculptural, potential of glass. The leading figures in this development were almost exclusively North American, and included Dominick Labino, Harvey K Littleton and Sam Herman. It was the discovery in 1962 by Labino, an artist and scientist, of a special formula for glass which became molten at a relatively low temperature which opened up new horizons for glassmaking. His discovery

(LEFT) *The Italian flair for design dominated the post-war years.*

(RIGHT) *Bowl consisting of spiralling threads of blue and brown glass designed by Vicke Lindstrand for the Swedish glassworks Kosta (c.1955).*

(BELOW) *A selection of glass by the celebrated Italian firm of Venini & Co. produced during the 1960s.*

allowed a sufficient quantity of material for a single item to be worked in a small kiln which could be easily accommodated in the average studio or classroom. The furnace had to be specially designed to be compact, cheap and able to run on bottled propane gas. Only then could glassblowing break away from the industrial base which had previously been necessary to house the elaborate and expensive equipment hitherto required. This enabled a growing number of individual craftsmen/ artists/designers and art colleges to extend their creative capabilities and explore the limitless potential of glass as a creative medium.

The United States had benefited from the sudden influx of Europe's avant-garde, who had fled the ravages of war at home. In addition to many of the Bauhaus teachers, mature artists such as Fernand Léger, Marc Chagall and Max Ernst introduced challenging ideas and stimulated new directions. It was a period of increased cross-fertilization between artists of different mediums. Traditional barriers were being challenged and broken down to foster a more enlightened perspective. This, in turn, provoked a reassessment of the role of the artist-craftsman.

In glass, it was no longer sufficient to be a chemist evolving formulae, an artisan working by the furnace and a designer exploring new techniques – the new craftsman also had to nurture an affinity within the rarefied world of the fine arts.

(ABOVE) *Inspired perhaps by the later work of Marinot, the Dutch artist Andries Dirk Copier has concentrated on internal composition of this vessel using iridization and entrapped air to dramatic effect (c.1951).*

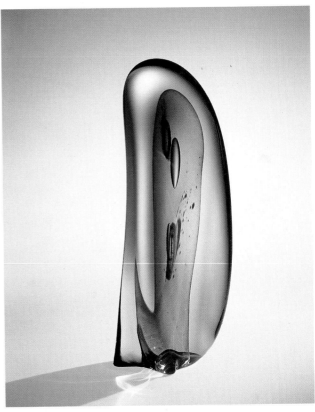

(ABOVE) *Untitled sculpture (1969) by Dominick Labino, who was a pioneer of the Studio Glass Movement within America, featuring air traps and gold veiling; (height 11in/275mm).*

American individualism

This new revival of the hand-crafted object, however, had little to do with William Morris's Utopian vision of the working man. Its primary role was to satisfy the growing demand for unique, one-off pieces, particularly by the wealthy few, who bought such work often only to boost their self-image. The necessary infrastructure, namely magazines, museums, retail outlets and exhibitions, grew in tandem with the crafts revival. In New York, for example, the American Craftsmen's Council, the Museum of Contemporary Crafts and the shop 'America House' had all become firmly established institutions by the early 1960s.

The new direction within glass was labelled the International Studio Glass Movement and its foremost exponent was, and probably still is, Harvey K Littleton, who was born in the home of American glass production, Corning, in New York State. Initially a ceramist, he spent some time studying glass production in Europe before setting up his own workshop in 1962. At the time he was one of only a small handful of men who worked glass by hand at the edge of the furnace. It was during the American Craftsmen's Council conference held at

(LEFT) *Varied selection of free-formed glass from the 1950s and 60s by the Italian firm of Venini & Co.; a vetro sommerso bird, a pezzato vase and a double-neck vase.*

The highly coloured glass of Paolo Venini is often cited as quintessentially 1960s. His work, however, merits closer study because it possesses not only a lively spontaneity, but also an elusive elegance not found in other glass artists of the period. Historically, Venini's contribution is also important because it was he who, along with Giacomo Cappellin, was responsible for shaking Venice from its lethargy in the early part of this century. The city had slept through the influential Arts and Crafts revolution which had swept through most other parts of Europe and it was not until the 1920s that the Venetians finally awoke to the new dynamism within the arts generally, and glass in particular.

THE FROZEN MOMENT

During the late 1960s the American-born Sam Herman became a leading figure in British glass design. His influence was considerable not only as a practitioner but also as a teacher. He himself was once a gifted pupil of Harvey K. Littleton and his own students at the Royal College of Art were soon to become the nucleus of British glass artists for the forthcoming decade. Herman's unique contribution to 20th century glass was his ability to capture the mercurial magic of glass in its liquid state, to freeze the metal in its state of flux. The two examples on the left are of cased glass embedded with multi-coloured streaks.

Lake George, New York, in 1959 that Littleton first put forward the revolutionary concept that '. . . glass should be a medium for the individual artist'. This seemingly obvious statement was to have far-reaching implications for the entire profession.

Littleton's challenge was accepted by the Toledo Museum of Art in Ohio, who offered facilities and funds and invited him and Dominick Labino, who at the time was research vice-president of Johns-Manville Fiber Glass Corporation, to organize two practical seminars on glassmaking in 1962. The following year, Littleton was able to convince the University of Wisconsin at Madison, where he had been a tutor since 1951, to enrol students into what was to be the first Studio Glass degree course. Momentum quickly picked up and there were soon dozens of colleges and universities offering studio glass as part of their fine arts curriculum.

Littleton's own work in glass has explored a wide range of techniques, yet always retained a sense of spontaneity and dynamism. He has created a prodigious number of hand-blown glass sculptures, which have sometimes been classified as Abstract Expressionism. He would eschew such a convenient label and would instead prefer to discuss the inherent qualities of reflection, transparency, immediacy, pliancy and absorption. His pioneering work has also been at the fore in the two major exhibitions, separated by 20 years, which have provided a definitive picture of the International Studio Glass Movement: the first, in 1959, marked its introduction as a mainstream art form alongside painting and sculpture, while the second, in 1979, consolidated its new role as a vehicle for pure art.

'Glass 1959 – A Special Exhibition of International Contemporary Glass' was premièred at the Corning

(LEFT) Foursquare *by Harvey K Littleton, whose individual energy and enthusiasm gave rise to the Studio Glass Movement.*

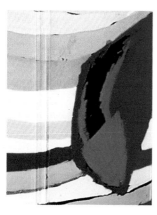

(ABOVE AND ABOVE RIGHT)
Spaceman (c.1955) by the Italian artist Gino Colucci exhibiting a colourful fusion of psychedelic imagery and Pop Art.

Museum of Glass in New York and was especially significant because it was the first time examples of contemporary studio glass had been brought together for a major critical overview. In total, some 2,000 items had been submitted for consideration, many of which had originated from small specialized studios operating under the sponsorship of larger, more established firms such as Steuben in the United States, Orrefors in Sweden and Rosenthal in Germany. The majority of the objects exhibited were essentially functional in spirit, although there was a pronounced leaning by some towards the sculptural. This tendency was played down in the official catalogue in which Edgar Kaufman, Jr, wrote that '. . . I am no friend to extravagant compositions in glass. As sculpture or as a field for the graven image, in the sense of the fine arts, glass seems woefully forced. Twentieth century glass seems to me nobly represented in the Pyrex dish . . .'

Only 20 years later, his words were to ring very hollow. The Studio Glass Movement had by 1979 proved its ability to transcend the functional and instead probe the abstract nature of the non-representational in glass. The 1979 exhibition, 'New Glass – A Worldwide Survey', premièred again at Corning before commencing an extended tour, and must still rate as the most comprehensive selection to date. Examples of work submitted for consideration had trebled since 1959 to over 6,000, and the global significance of the new movement was reflected in the number of participating countries, some 28 in all, with the United States still the largest contributor, followed by Czechoslovakia and Germany. Erwin Eisch (b. 1927), one of the leading European figures, aptly summed up this new spirit by describing how '. . . the Art Nouveau glass artists were concerned primarily with vessel forms . . . but for me a vessel cannot serve as an artistic point of departure; my primary concerns are pure three-dimensional form, glass as a medium for expression, and an art for its own functionless sake.'

(ABOVE) *Pair of decanters (1962) in blue-grey glass, manufactured in Finland. Mass-produced Finnish glass has been exported worldwide for decades.*

(RIGHT) *Untitled piece from the Johansfors Series (1974) by the American glass artist Michael E. Taylor; (height 8½in/207mm, width 16½in/410mm).*

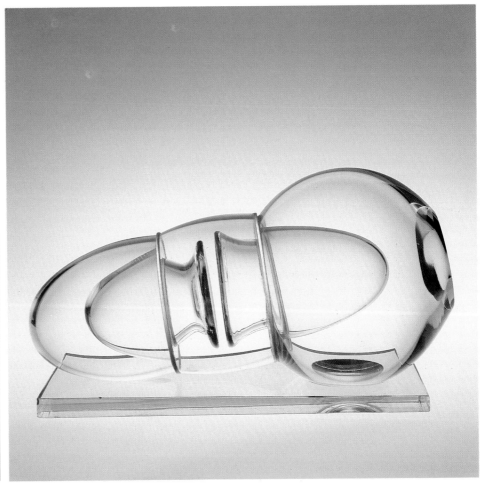

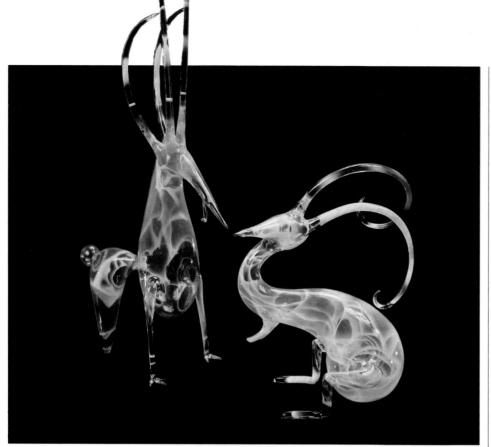

(LEFT) *Capricorn and Deer (c.1965) by the Czech Jaroslav Brychta comes perilously close to being labelled Kitsch.*

(RIGHT)*Orchid Vase (1954) by Timo Sarpaneva for the leading Finnish glassworks of Iittala, who have also manufactured glass for the architect Alvar Aalto; (height 13½in/ 343mm).*

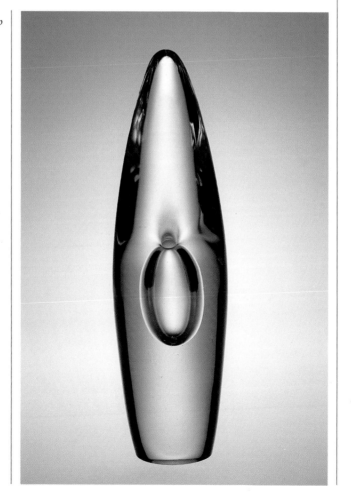

EISCH

. . . .

'The essential Rules of the Material'

Eisch, a German artist, was the first European to work solo in hot glass; his earliest one-man show was held in Stuttgart in June 1962. His family had enjoyed a long association with the manufacture of glass and his early apprenticeship ably equipped him in the traditional skills of the glassblower. It was his studies in sculpture at the Academy of Art in Munich, however, which sparked the imagination:

> . . . the experience of three-dimensional form brought me out of the confined atmosphere of two-dimensional designing. The expression of the material shaped by the hands, the mind and the spirit – this brought me a great freedom and unfolding of the creative nature. I soon discovered that one does not discover new forms and ideas only in the conventional method of design – by drawing the designs.

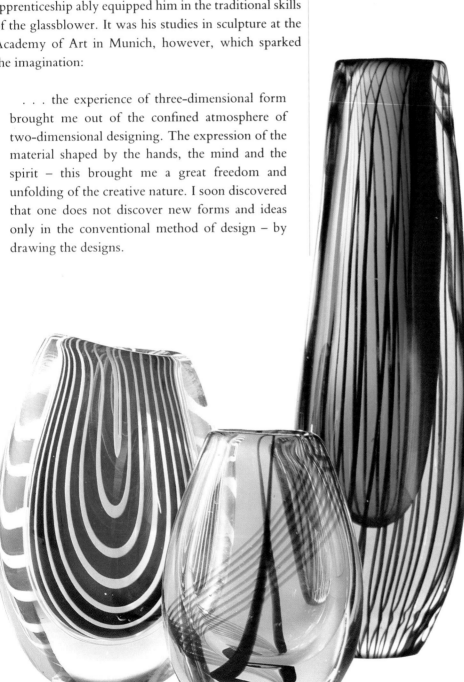

(RIGHT) *Telephon (1971) by Erwin Eisch of the Federal Republic of Germany, who was the foremost glass artist of the Pop Art movement.*

(LEFT) *Three vases (c.1960) designed by Vicke Lindstrand (b.1904) who rose to prominence initially with the Swedish company of Orrefors Glasbruk, between the years 1928–41, before moving on to the Kosta Glassworks in 1950. In his role there as chief designer he experimented with a wide variety of techniques including prismatic cutting, engraving and Iatticinio. His most successful work involves abstract, amorphous shapes which are shot through with swirling lines of intense colour.*

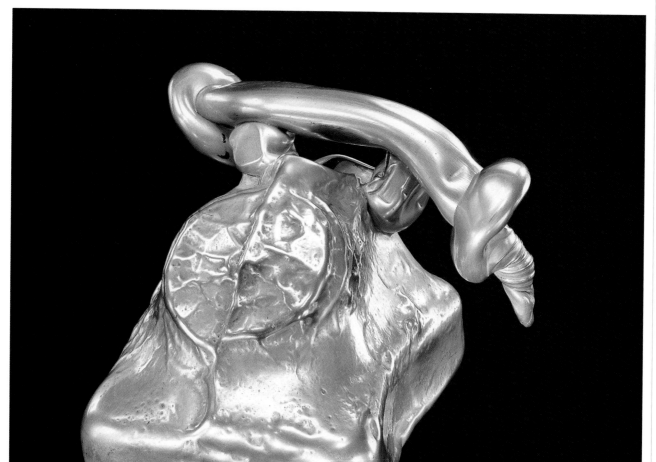

Being an informed young man in the 1960s, Erwin Eisch possessed a natural empathy for the ideas of the Pop Art movement. His innate belief in the freedom of expression made him ideally qualified to become an unofficial spokesperson for the burgeoning New Wave Studio Glass movement, whose principal ideas he summarized in a lecture given to the Deutscher Glastechnische Gesellschaft in October 1975: 'We must recognize the essential rules of the material, respect them and work within them. We are interested only in the result of our work. The fluid material must receive breath, meaning and form – a form that for us clarifies and reflects the spirit of our time.'

The initial rush of excitement which was sustained through the 1960s has subsequently matured somewhat and is today more mellow, more calculated. Most of the major founding fathers are still practising; Harvey Littleton, Marvin Lipofsky (b. 1938), Dale Chihuly (b. 1941), André Billéci (b. 1933) and many others. Their numbers have, of course, been swelled by the massive expansion in the art-college system and the increasing number of talented students attracted to the inherent qualities of glass as an expressive medium.

This new-found enthusiasm continues to grow and has been carefully nurtured by a succession of expansive exhibitions in several major cities around the world, including 'Contemporary Glass – Europe and Japan' in Tokyo, 'Today's Glass, Art or Craft?' in Zürich and 'American Glass Now' in Toledo. These, in turn, have been supplemented by a sustained growth within the commercial gallery circuit which provides a valuable shop window for the latest developments and offers the budding collector an ideal opportunity to be extravagant with his or her money.

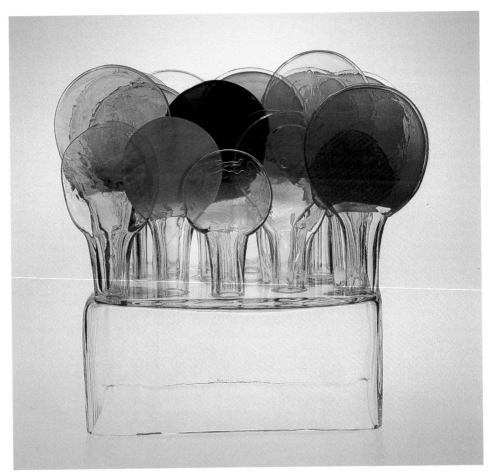

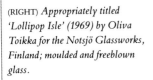

(RIGHT) *Appropriately titled 'Lollipop Isle' (1969) by Oliva Toikka for the Notsjö Glassworks, Finland; moulded and freeblown glass.*

Italy

The excitement of the contemporary glass scene and the prominent position of glass as a valid art form is equally true in Europe, where several eminent glass-houses have been consistently breaking new ground since the late 1940s. This is particularly so in Italy, which for many years has been considered the quintessence of style and elegance in both glass and design generally. Italy's great natural storehouse of cultural and artistic heritage has stirred many native talents to aspire to greatness and achieve pre-eminence in almost every sphere of design. The critic Umberto Eco endeavoured to explain this phenomenon thus: '. . . if other countries have had a theory of design, Italy has had a philosophy of design, maybe even an ideology'.

The most important figures in the development of Italian glass originated, of course, from Murano. This small island, a few miles from Venice, had been the home of Venetian glass since the 13th century, when the furnaces were moved out of the city for fear of the spread of fire. The secrets of each glasshouse have been handed down to succeeding generations of the same family. By doing so they have fortunately sustained a creative network of small workshops linked by a continuing respect for the craft tradition and an inherent passion for the material itself.

The success of the Salviati workshops during the late 19th century (discussed in Chapter Two) relied exclusively on Antonio Salviati's use of historical quotations. Past eras were sifted through again and again to embellish the banal and seduce the weary consumer. Italy's defeat at the hands of the Allied Forces, however, finally uprooted the industry's ambivalent attitude towards the modern age, and signalled a new approach to both design and manufacture.

Paolo Venini (1895–1959), originally descended from an ancient glassblowing family from Como, was the first to embrace this new concept wholeheartedly. His early years had been spent as a lawyer, but then in the 1920s, saddened by the crass vulgarity of much that was labelled contemporary Murano glassware, he decided to channel his energies into the medium of glass. He

(BOTTOM RIGHT) *Venini Vaso a Carre and Spicchi bottle vase; Archimede Seguso vase (right).*

bought into the Rioda Glassworks and devoted his time to the study of both the technical and the artistic difficulties in producing high quality glassware. Concentrating at first on traditional images inspired by early oil paintings, he broke away in 1926 to form a new firm, Venini & Co, which would allow him the freedom to experiment with unusual surface treatments and innovative techniques, and to employ challenging new designers such as Gio Ponti and, later, Salvador Dali.

(BELOW) *Cire-perdue alive and well, 1953 (see page 62): Diatretum vase by American Frederick Carder (diameter 7in/18cm).*

Venini not only possessed a great artistic vision but also considerable personal integrity, craftsmanship and creativity. His technical achievements included the development of numerous forms of ornamental glass, including *vetro battuto*, literally, 'beaten glass'; *vetro corroso*, 'corroded glass'; *vetro occhi*, 'glass with eyes'; *vetro pennelato*, 'painted glass'; *vetro pizzo*, 'lace glass', and *vetro pulegoso*, 'bubbled glass'. His most celebrated pieces were a range of bowls from the 1950s, which were given the generic term of 'handkerchief bowls' because of their resemblance to the loose folds of a cupped handkerchief.

Venini's principal rival at Murano was the firm of Barovier & Toso, which was formed in 1936 by descendants of two of Murano's oldest glassmaking families, namely, the brothers Artemio and Decio Toso, and

(BELOW) *Composizione Astratta (1955) by Angelo Barovier; height 60in/1502mm, width 40in/1002mm.*

(BELOW RIGHT) *Model of stained-glass window for the rebuilding of Coventry Cathedral. A collaborative venture between two Englishmen, John Piper the designer and Patrick Reytiens the maker.*

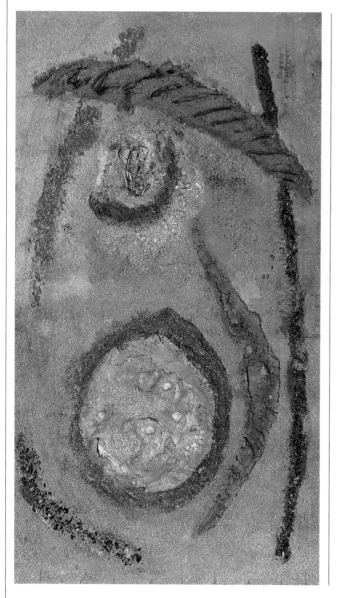

(ABOVE) *Sleeping Bird (c.1961) by Timo Sarpaneva for the Iittala Glassworks.*

Ercole Barovier (1884–1974). They recognized the significant changes which the growth in mass-consumption would entail. A sophisticated design philosophy was therefore formulated, in conjunction with an ongoing programme of technical developments which led to several new types of decorative glass such as *vetro aborigene*, or 'primitive glass'; *vetro barbarico*, 'barbarous glass'; *vetro diafano*, 'diaphanous glass'; *vetro gemmato*, 'gem-like glass'; *vetro primavera*, 'spring-time glass' and *vetro rugiadoso*, 'dew-like glass'.

The highly finished nature of such glass was essential if it was to appeal to its intended clientele, that is, the wealthy, cosmopolitan middle classes. The use of bold colours and sculptural shapes, which symbolized the expressive nature of 1950s glass, was dominated by four major firms: Vetri d'Arte, Venini, Fontane Arte and

Barovier & Toso. Between them, these four Italian companies had succeeded in bridging the gap between the craft tradition and the modern age without necessarily forfeiting the special environment of the artisans' workshop, nor adopting the overtly commercial practices of, say, many firms in the United States. They also provided Italy with an important source of foreign exchange and enjoyed the 'Economic Miracle' of the period 1950 to 1963, which saw sustained financial growth both within Italy and the newly formed European Economic Community.

This sudden upward surge in the marketplace of the consumer eventually gave rise to an ideological crisis of confidence within the design world. The object was now looked down upon as nothing more than commercial greed, dictated by the whim of the consumer – in effect, a symbol of base materialistic gain. Design was vilified as élitist and rejected as being remote from the ongoing struggles of the real world. The widespread student unrest of the late 1960s eventually spilled over into the design world, toppling the tables of the comfortable, the complacent and the conceited and consequently calling for a new direction, a new blueprint, a new design.

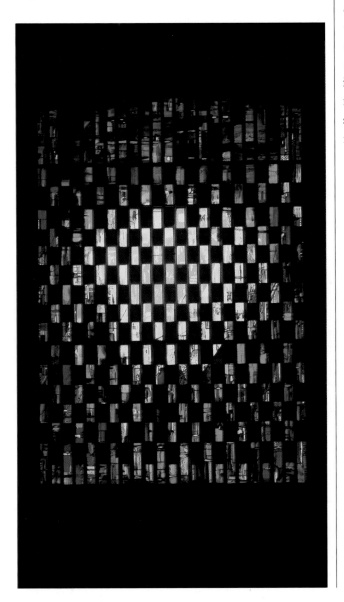

7

New Design and the Vigorously Eclectic

The cutting edge of glass in the 1980s Jen Sidej Carafe by Borek Sipek.

The fragmentation of accepted notions, which followed on from the political turmoil of the late 1960s, was a direct consequence of the explosion of information and ideas which was to typify the new age of mass communications. The late 1970s witnessed the beginning of a flood of satellite televisions, photocopiers, facsimile machines, video machines, desk-top computers and international dialling codes which was to hasten the demise of the Modernist's heroic vision and the emergence of an eclectic, cultural pluralism.

National frontiers were quietly, but steadily, erased as the electronic media revolution gathered pace. The homogeneity within design, which was for so long the bedrock of Modernism, was now seen to be irrevocably flawed. What was once rational and heroic was now fragmented and discordant. The glib cliché 'Form follows Function', once honoured as the canon of Modernity, now rang hollow. Function, which was once so simple and so clear, was now discussed in terms of cultural conditioning and historical events. The polemicist designer Ettore Sottsass, Jr (b. 1917), realized that '. . . when you try to define the function of any object, the function slips through your fingers because function is life itself. Function is not one screw more or one measure less. Function is the final possibility of the relation between an object and life.'

(ABOVE) *Uncharacteristically monochromatic glass vase (1978) by Ettore Sottsass, the doyen of the new dynamism within Italian design.*

(LEFT) *Glass sculpture (1970) by Marvin Lipofsky, an early pioneer of the Studio Glass Movement within America.*

Such pervasive and radical restructuring of ideas has been a characteristic feature of the post-World War II era. The American critic Frederic Jameson established this new consensus in his perceptive essay, 'Post-Modernism and the Consumer Society', written in 1983, in which he analyzed this '. . . new kind of society, variously described as post-industrial society, multi-national capitalism, consumer society, media society . . .

(ABOVE AND RIGHT) *Vrosikutiot (1978–87) by Oliva Toikka for the Notzjö Glassworks, Finland.*

THE PRAGUE SPRING

(RIGHT) *Bird Platter (1979) by Ivo Rozsypal; (diameter 14in/356mm)*

(BELOW) *Black Spirit (1986) by Dana Zamecnikova.*

The Czechoslovak nation achieved full independence only in 1918 but the age-old traditions of Bohemian glass for quality and craftsmanship were vigorously maintained. The glassmaking industry was later nationalized in 1948 and continued to produce some of the most original glass of the post-war era. This success was largely due to the comprehensive reorganization of both the industry and the educational system. This process of nationalization positively encouraged diversity and experimentation. The Ministry of Culture quickly realized the valuable contribution talented young artists could make on the international scene and the other Bohemian glassworks have now been augmented by new factories at Novy Bor, Zelesny, Skrdlovice and Karlovy Vary.

new types of consumption, planned obsolescence, an ever rapid rhythm of fashion and styling changes, the penetration of advertising, television and media generally to a hitherto unparalleled degree throughout society; . . . these are some of the features which seem to mark a radical break with that old pre-war society in which high modernism was still an underground force.'

Modernism claimed the validity of the perfect solution: the one truth. This was the same truth which Henry Ford strove for in offering the great American public *one* standard motor-car, the 'Model T' Ford, available in '. . . any colour as long as it's black'. Such an arrogant denial of cultural tradition and individual taste inevitably eroded away and eventually gave rise to the Post-Modern. The phrase trips off the tongue: but what does it mean?

Subversive derivation

The Post-Modernists adopted a sceptical, somewhat subversive view of the modern age. They looked upon design not as a soberly scientific process governed by the dictates of utility and ergonomics, but as an artistic activity where the imagination was fired by the vagaries of historical memory. This process not only courted the irreverent and the transgressive but also the irrelevant and the banal. The artist was free to lazily wander at random through the pages of history, expanding, or amending, where necessary to afford him any and every opportunity for imitation, quotation and even pastiche. This fusion of new/old ideas denied the cult of originality, arguing instead that the term 'innovation' was a mis-nomer and that all new art was, in fact, a derivative of past art. Debate focused on the sterility of Modernism and the problem of enthusing a general public which was becoming increasingly cosmopolitan, visually literate and more in touch with the social and cultural changes occurring within a broad spectrum of society.

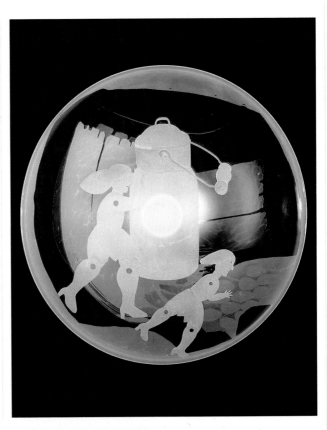

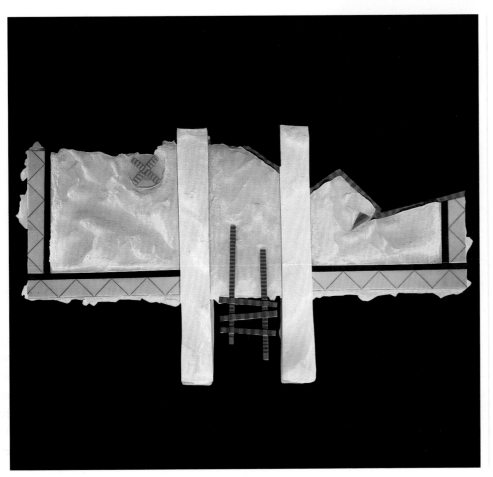

(ABOVE) *The Milky Way (1979) by Swedish artist Ann Wärff; (diameter 15½in/390mm).*

(LEFT) Druid Site No. 43 *(1986) by Australian artist Warren Langley; (height 20in/508mm, width 38in/950mm)*

The difficulties of capturing the attention of such an informed and aware potential clientele was hindered by the plethora of mass-media images. This necessitated the development of a more wilfully brash approach to design which could unsettle the public's predictable response to a table, a chair or a vase. It was the object which was now the principal totem of the design world, not the grand city plan or the apartment block.

New attention-getting tactics included clashing colours of vivid hues, combining materials of a seemingly contradictory nature, fusing shapes into decidedly bizarre forms and generating surface patterns possessing a deceptively random energy. Glass was an ideal medium for such new ideas. This new awareness was also intended to help break down the traditional barriers between the different professional bodies: furniture design, graphic design, product design, interior design, urban design and architecture were all receptive to this new trend, wherein the emphasis was on form over function, content over form, symbolism over content.

Advocates of this new approach argued that design was not suspended in a vacuum, it was not just an empty receptacle, but it existed within a complex framework of cultural references and social values. It was imperative that these should be acknowledged and, where possible, challenged or even celebrated. Developments in the fields of structuralism, linguistics, semantics and semiology (the science of signs) provided the

(RIGHT) Alcor *(1983) by Ettore Sottsass; (height 18½in/464mm, diameter 7in/182mm).*

(LEFT) Sirio *(1982) by Ettore Sottsass; both vases were manufactured by Tosso Vetri d'Arte for the Milan-based avant-garde design group Memphis; (height 14in/358mm, diameter 5½in/ 141mm).*

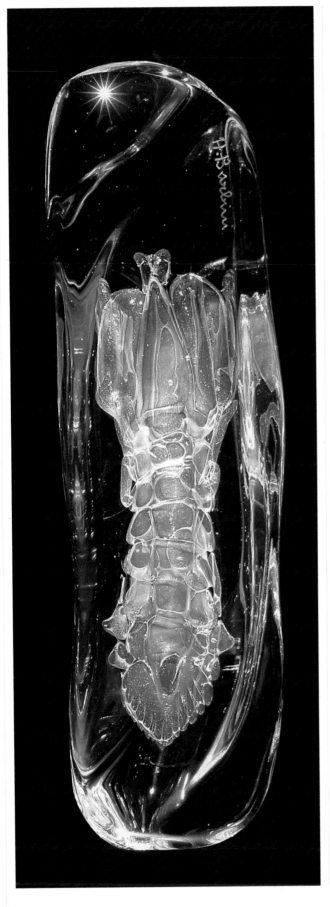

necessary intellectual springboard for this new movement, which looked upon design as a 'series of accidents', charged with symbolism and association, and as a system of signs, allowing multiple meanings to be layered one on top of another. Sottsass elaborated on this point and reasoned: 'Anything that is tamed by culture loses its flavour after a while, it's like eating cardboard. You have to put mustard on it or take little pieces of cardboard and eat them with tomatoes and salad. It's a lot better if you don't eat cardboard at all.'

Italy was the initial breeding ground of this now global dissatisfaction. As a country she had endured some 15 years of intense cultural and intellectual debate, sparked off by the political upheaval which had occurred during the late 1960s. The bustling, industrial city of Milan, in the prosperous north, was the home of several Post-Radical architect/designers who, during the period from 1978 to 1980, operated under the collective title Studio Alchymia. They included the influential figures of Sottsass, Andrea Branzi, Michele de Lucchi, Alessandro Mendini and Paola Navone. Their shared goal was to literally reinvent design and overturn the accepted notions of polite 'good taste'.

Studio Alchymia explored uncharted areas of the banal and the kitsch, undergoing a metamorphosis in the winter of 1980–81 to be reborn as Memphis. The name Memphis was appropriate because of the conflicting associations; not only Elvis Presley, Blues music, Tennessee and the American South, but also Egypt and the fabled city of the pharaohs. It was, in fact, lifted from a Bob Dylan song called 'Stuck Outside of Mobile with the Memphis Blues Again'. The group was primarily made up of architects and comprized Ettore Sottsass and Michele de Lucchi, along with Marco Zanini, Aldo Cibic, Matteo Thun, George J Sowden, Nathalie du Pasquier, Martine Bedin and the critic Barbara Radice.

(LEFT) Crustacean *(c.1985) by Italian artist Alfredo Baicbisci, manipulated while hot to create air traps; (height 13½in/337mm).*

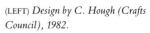

(RIGHT) *Asymmetrical scent bottles by F Tookey (Crafts Council of Great Britain) with hot glass decoration.*

(LEFT) *Design by C. Hough (Crafts Council), 1982.*

Their early collaborations enjoyed the support of a select number of celebrated Post-Modern architects, including Hans Hollein of Austria and Michael Graves of the United States. Their first show in September 1981, however, caused a storm of controversy which quickly swept across the globe. The seemingly garbled cacophony of awkward shapes, incongruous materials, bold patterns and bold colours shocked everyone who was there for opening night.

It was Sottsass who provided the intellectual rigour to justify their radical approach. He argued that 'I am an idiot and always say that the problem is to eat, to drink, to have sex, to stay low, low, low. The world is a sensorial recovery zone. I'm not discussing a configuration but an attitude.'

This attitude which Sottsass describes relies upon the analysis of design via one's senses, not one's intellect. The Memphis philosophy or 'New Design' (to give it its generic title) shuns the Post-Modernist's recidivistic recycling of past styles. New Design rejects the past and instead explores an eclectic collage of ambiguous imagery gleaned from today's society. It sifts through the mass of disparate messages vying for attention to create a fusion of the popular with the visionary.

(RIGHT) Breakwater *(1976) by Eino Maelt of the Union of Soviet Socialist Republics; (height 7in/ 174mm).*

(BELOW) *Selection of diverse glass objets d'art (c.1985) by Diana Hobson, Tim Shaw and Arlon Bayliss.*

The seduction of instability

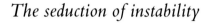

The ability of New Design to tackle the concept of built-in redundancy was outlined in 1984 by Barbara Radice, in a collection of essays brought out to accompany a Canadian exhibition entitled 'Phoenix – New Attitudes in Design'. In it she argued that

> While digging into the complex texture of existence, New Design does not stop to decipher it, to formulate it, to fix it in a framework; it does not offer solutions or certainties; rather it tries to tune itself to the rhythms of a permanent creative restlessness and to the quiet ripples of our own inevitable metamorphosis; it offers itself to total and immediate consumption. It makes metaphors, shortens the time and, moving on to other things, maintains the suspense. It does not try to convince but to seduce, and it seduces precisely because of its enigmatic and contradictory qualities: because of its total dedication to instability, to the representation of provisional, evanescent, impregnable states. It seduces because of its supreme indifference toward problems of solidity, stability, continuity; it seduces because it refuses to define things and to define itself.' Its seductions, if successful, are striking, total, sudden, and final.

(ABOVE) *Study in natural form in stained glass by British artist Paul Quail, whose commissions include windows for Coventry Cathedral.*

This quotation characterizes the new attitudes within design: unconventional, jagged and informed. The 1970s might be marginalized as uninspired, insecure and introspective; the 1980s may well be remembered as confused, abrasive and ironic.

The burgeoning Post-Modern movement within design, and architecture in particular, has enjoyed considerable popularity of late. Its principal role, however, is to legitimize the plundering of earlier societies and antiquated styles in order to provide a framework of ready-made motifs for those uncertain of success. The critic Julian Gibb sketched out the basic intellectual parameters of the Post-Modernist thus: 'Post-Modernism relegates rationalism, including reductivism, and material and formal economy to positions of low priority *in order to* expand the factors of *humanitarian concern* and *meaning* in functional artifacts, returning those factors to the position which they once occupied in pre-mechanised, pre-industrialised society and which they *still* occupy in those cultures not yet invaded by industrialisation; for example, primal societies.'

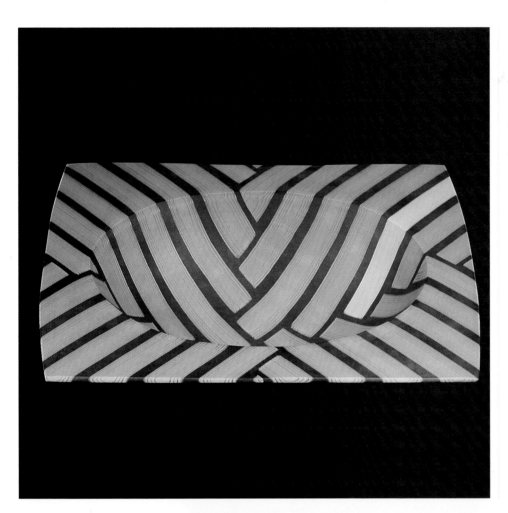

(LEFT) Gold *(1980) by Klaus Moje of the Federal Republic of Germany. A mosaic bowl formed by fusing rods of different coloured glass within a shaped mould. Surface imperfections can be removed by grinding after the piece has cooled, but it is a difficult process requiring great technical skill.*

(RIGHT) Bowl *(1978) by Gunter Knye of the German Democratic Republic; (height 4½in/109mm, diameter 7½in/193mm).*

The above quotations provide a poignant illustration of the divergent paths within design in the 1980s. The fragmentation of earlier dogmas has encouraged fresh ideas and has been instrumental in evolving a vigorously eclectic approach to the use of glass. The 'rediscovery' of the Cubist technique of collage has opened up new horizons for the artist and many of the younger designers currently exploring such methods have also taken to using glass as a means of extending their vocabulary. They often collaborate with one of the larger glass factories to manufacture limited-production runs of items which are aggressively contemporary, yet also provide some continuity for an age-old tradition.

Several of the Memphis group, notably Sottsass and Zanini, have benefited from Italy's unique infrastructure of small family-run workshops to experiment with vividly coloured glass in novel forms, creating objects which simultaneously shock and intrigue. The bizarre shapes, although seemingly illogical, are in fact, underpinned by a rigorous intellectual framework, and push the usual notions of good taste to new limits.

(LEFT) Wall Paper Panel *by the American Molly Stone (1983). Fused, kiln-formed and laminated; (height 29½in/76cm).*

(BELOW) *Danny Lane's hard-edged interior installation comprising bar, tables and chairs; for the Moscow Club, 62 Frith Street, London. The bar is 35ft/10.5m long, and cut and polished 1in/25mm float glass supported by ¼-inch welded plate steel.*

'Prepared to be hurt'

Another designer who has formally rejected the traditional associations of glass is the American Danny Lane. Born in 1955 in Urbana, Illinois, Danny Lane has lived and worked in London since the mid-1970s. His radical (mis)use of glass is both highly original and highly unorthodox. His work exhibits a rare creative tension which threatens our conventional prejudices about what glass can and cannot do, thus exposing our reluctance to accept glass as more than simply a decorative or applied art. He believes that '. . . in order to create really beautiful objects one needs to be open, accessible, prepared to be hurt, otherwise certain experiences are not easily understood'.

Lane's uncompromising attitude derives from an insatiable appetite for conflict, both emotive and physical. He welcomes any potential adversity to provide the necessary creative spark to motivate his work. He originally went to Great Britain to study stained glass under the guidance of the artist Patrick Reyntiens (b. 1925), who had earlier collaborated with John Piper on the stained glass for the rebuilding of Coventry's Cathedral.

In the mid-1970s, Lane moved on to the Central School of Art to study painting and it was at this time that the excitement of the originally British Punk philosophy in music and fashion spilled over onto the streets of London, extolling nihilism, anarchy and destruction. Lane's less refined pieces display a certain affinity with the Punk aesthetic and underline the perfidious nature of the material itself – the broken plane, the scratched surface, the jagged edge.

(LEFT) *Romeo and Juliet Table by Danny Lane, an American-born designer whose clear intention is to subvert conventional notions of how glass should be used.*

(RIGHT) *Detail of Mobile Screen (1987) Danny Lane, consisting of 23 interlocking pieces of sand-blasted ½in/10mm thick tempered glass; (height 11ft/3.3m, width 10ft/3m).*

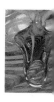

NORTHERN LIGHTS

Throughout the 1960s Scandinavian design was the benchmark of 'good taste'. The clean lines and common-sense detailing appealed particularly to countries such as Britain and the United States, who had lost their sense of purpose with the collapse of Modernism. Sweden's neutrality during World War II allowed her native designers to develop their burgeoning ideas unhindered by the threat of military service. The two largest glasshouses, Kosta (founded in 1742) and Orrefors (founded in 1726), had embarked on an ambitious expansion programme which entailed the recruitment of talented artists such as Sven Palmqvist, Vicke Lindstrand, Edvin Öhrström and Ann Wärff. The inspiration of such figures only increased Sweden's already considerable skill in free-form glassblowing and fine engraving, and thus ensured their continuing success in world markets.

(LEFT) *Decanter with stopper housing small goblet (c.1983) manufactured by the Swedish company Kosta.*

His candour is such that he openly states about his work: 'It wasn't designed, it just happened . . . I'm not a designer's designer. I'm more about expression and telling a story. It has been pointed out to me that I'm very English.' This admission provides an additional key to understanding his maverick character, but equally important is his enduring admiration for the glass artist Patrick Reyntiens, who has often been labelled the 'quintessential Englishman' – principally because of his modest, self-deprecating attitude towards his art and his thirst for hard work and self-discipline. In 1983, Lane established a bona fide workshop/showroom in London called 'The Glassworks' to help promote innovative glass within a somewhat conservative British market and to provide a retail outlet for his idiosyncratic, one-off items of domestic furniture: screens, tables, chairs and the like.

(LEFT) *Two champagne glasses by Borek Sipek, manufactured by the Milanese glassworks Sawaya & Moroni.*

Sipek has worked with glass for many years now and approaches each new commission as a personal journey of discovery. Much of his work explores the historical and cultural traditions of glass, whereby the given both informs and limits each particular project. One such recent project, entitled *Vase, Vasa, Vasi*, involved the design and manufacture of seven different vases in seven different countries. This challenging schedule involved travelling to each country – Czechoslovakia, Japan, France, India, Mexico, England and Egypt – working closely with an unfamiliar manufacturer and coping with an unknown city and the foreign language. The resultant vases were a culmination of these disparate forces.

(RIGHT) Skoro nic: *fruit bowl by the Czech-born architect/designer Borek Sipek.*

Sipek: Contemporary Craftsman

An equally talented designer is the Czech émigré, Borek Sipek. Sipek was born in Prague in 1949, but now operates from a base in Amsterdam. His university education covered a broad spectrum of interests: furniture at Prague; architecture at Hamburg and finally philosophy at Stuttgart. This breadth of thought is reflected in the complexity of his work and the diversity of his interests. His quest for knowledge is not manifest in his intellect alone, but is informed by his considerable practical skills as a craftsman. He is not only an accomplished glass-blower but has also worked in metal, timber, marble, ceramics and silk. Working with such a wide spectrum of materials has afforded him the opportunity to expand the traditional view of the 'craftsman'. His work in glass, while aggressively modern, possesses great invention and creative vigour. The majority of pieces are produced in his native Czechoslovakia, in the factory of Novy Bor, situated near Prague. He sees his work as a 'dialogue between geometric and organic form' and believes that 'functionalism must inform design at the beginning, while material should ornament and adorn it'.

INTO THE WHIRLPOOL

This is a complex work involving a great variety of different techniques, including sandblasting, polishing, copper electro-forming and blowing. The use of copper produces either a turquoise, green or red hue depending upon the temperature of the furnace. This knowledge is by no means new and was exploited by the glassmakers of ancient Egypt. Sand blasting, however, was only invented in 1870 by an American chemist named Benjamin Tilghman. It can generate a finely pitted or frosted effect which can be carefully controlled according to the type of abrasive used (sand, powdered iron or flint, for example) and the force with which it is expelled. A protective mask is used to limit the effect to within the desired area.

(RIGHT) *Maelstrom (1981) by American artist Michael M. Glancy; (diameter 7½in/ 185mm).*

The individual and highly personal nature of the above recent work reflects the current vitality within the applied arts generally, and glass in particular. Pieces of this calibre challenge accepted stereotypes and subvert long-cherished notions of what may be considered beautiful or elegant. Charged with meaning and meta-phor, such work confronts issues which are relevant to

FROSTED RADIO LIGHT (1987)

This work is by American artist Paul Seide. The intense colours are achieved by charging the spirals of glass with neon and mercury vapour from a transmitted radio field; (height 19in/484mm, width 21½in/535mm).

society today. Numerous labels such as 'New Spirit', 'Post-Apocalyptic' or 'New Modern' have been invented in an effort to try and codify such innovative work. The strong tendency towards the sculptural in glass, however, denies such myopic classification and suggests that the current state of flux will no doubt continue for many years to come.

QUEEN IDA'S CHAIR (1986)

By American artist Keke Cribbs, a somewhat unconventional throne, but no more so than the eccentric furniture of the Italian designer of the 1920s and 30s, Carlo Buggati. This chair uses decorated glass, gilded clothes pegs, toy metal alligators and carved figures by Buffy Cribbs.

(LEFT) Spoke *(1986) by another American artist Karla Trinkley, in cast glass with hand-painted decoration; (height 12½in/310mm, diameter 15in/373mm).*

(RIGHT) Potato Landscape Pitcher *(1979) by American artist Richard Marquis. A deliberately provocative piece from the Fabricated Weird Series. When magnified, the solid white murrini spout reveals the legend: 'Chuck the duck/says life is/mostly hard work'. . . ? (diameter 4in/107mm).*

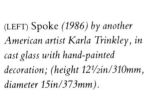

Index

Page numbers in *italic* refer to captions. Names
of works of art are followed by their date.

Picture credits

Bibliography

V Arwas *Glass – Art Nouveau to Art Deco* **Academy Editions** 1977.

P Bayer & M Waller *Lalique* **Bloomsbury** 1988.

G Beard *International Modern Glass* **Barrie & Jenkins** 1976.

A Branzi *The Hot House* **Thames & Hudson** 1984.

M Collins *Towards Post-Modernism* **British Museum** 1987.

F Cooke *Glass – Twentieth Century Design* **Bell & Hyman** 1986.

A Forty *Objects of Desire* **Thames & Hudson** 1986.

F Kaempfer & K Beyer *Glass – A World History* **Studio Vista** 1966.

K Middlemass *Continental Coloured Glass* **Barrie & Jenkins** 1971.

E Morris *Stained Glass* **Apple Press** 1988.

H Newman *Illustrated Dictionary of Glass* **Heineman** 1984.

N Pevsner *Pioneers of Modern Design* **Penguin** 1960.

P Phillips (ed.) *Encylopedia of Glass* **Heineman** 1981.

A Polak *Modern Glass* **Faber & Faber** 1962.

B Radice *Memphis* **Thames & Hudson** 1985.

W Warmus *Emile Gallé* **Corning** 1984.

H M Wingler *The Bauhaus* **MIT Press** 1978.